W9-DCB-643

WAR, PEACE AND JUSTICE

The Prophetic Record

John M. Swomley, Jr.

Copyright © 1985 by John M. Swomley, Jr.
Smith Grieves Company
All rights reserved by John M. Swomley, Jr.
Printed and bound in the United States of America

Copyright 1972 Christian Century Foundation. Reprinted by permission from the following issues of *The Christian Century:* June 28, 1967; October 30, 1968; December 27, 1972; September 25, 1974; September 29, 1976.

Copyright *Engage* and *Concern.* Reprinted by permission of *Engage*, United Methodist Board of Church and Society for the article in the May 15, 1971 issue of *Engage* and the article in the December 1, 1964 issue of *Concern.*

Copyright *Fellowship.* Reprinted by permission from the following issues of *Fellowship:* November 1945, December 1976, October 1977, April/May 1978, and April/May 1981. Nyack, New York.

Copyright *National Catholic Reporter.* Reprinted by permission of the *National Catholic Reporter,* P. O. Box 281, Kansas City, MO 64141, from the June 3, 1983 issue of the *National Catholic Reporter.*

Copyright *The Progressive.* Reprinted by permission of *The Progressive,* Madison, Wisconsin.

Copyright 1981 *The St. Luke's Journal of Theology.* Reprinted by permission, *The St. Luke's Journal of Theology,* The University of the South, Sewanee, TN 37375-4003, from the September 1981 issue.

Copyright *Zion's Herald.* Reprinted by permission from the December 26, 1951 issue of *Zion's Herald,* by The United Methodist Center.

Cover Design/Lew Heigham
Editor/Carl O. Bangs—A valued colleague of many years

This special limited edition is made possible by Saint Paul School of Theology, 5123 Truman Road, Kansas City, MO 64127.

In recognition of John Swomley as Professor Emeritus of Christian Ethics at Saint Paul School of Theology as of June, 1984.

CONTENTS

Introduction

The Second World War, which began in Europe in 1939, spread to the United States in 1941, and ended with the use of two atomic bombs in 1945, marked the beginning of a new and terrible epoch in world history. The author of this book was an active participant in the peace movement prior to World War II and the leading opponent of two post-war developments: the military-industrial complex and the effort to enact permanent universal military conscription.

During World War II he and his colleagues on the staff of the Fellowship of Reconciliation launched a movement of non-violent action against racial discrimination in northern and border cities which laid the groundwork for the Freedom Rides in the South and the movement led by Dr. Martin Luther King, Jr. The author also visited Japanese-American concentration camps and served as administrator of a program to re-settle Japanese Americans in Eastern and Midwestern communities.

Beginning in 1944 he worked in Washington as the director of a coalition of organizations formed to oppose conscription. The campaign was successful in defeating the conscription of labor and nurses in 1944-45 and universal military training in 1952. During those years in Washington he did the first research and writing about the planning and development of the military industrial complex, issuing a series of reports and booklets which he released to the press under the sponsorship of such persons as Albert Einstein, Pearl Buck, Dorothy Canfield Fisher, Victor Reuther, and Ray Lyman Wilbur.

As Executive Secretary of the Fellowship of Reconciliation from 1953 to 1960 he provided staff support and other assistance to Martin Luther King and his colleagues during the Montgomery Bus Boycott. He engaged in the first Christian-Communist dialogues, which were held in New York, arranged the release of several persons given indeterminate sentences during the McCarthyist period, and wrote numerous articles on disarmament, the cold war, militarism, the growth of American imperialism, and foreign policy.

In 1960 he came to Kansas City to teach Christian Social Ethics and the Philosophy of Religion in the Saint Paul School of Theology. He was frequently the center of controversy in Kansas City in the 1960s and early seventies but always with the support of his faculty colleagues and President Don W. Holter. His activities were chiefly in the field of racial justice, civil liberties, and peace, often as an adversary of the police, the American Legion, Civil Defense leaders, right wing organizations, and those advocating public aid to church schools and colleges. He was the first vocal opponent in Kansas City of the war in Vietnam and the first proponent of amnesty and of rights for selective conscientious objectors.

While on the faculty of the Saint Paul School of Theology he took sabbatical leaves to teach in graduate schools in Buenos Aires and Manila and in a black college during the guerrilla war in Rhodesia, now Zimbabwe. For many years he has served on the National Board and Executive Committee of the American Civil Liberties Union and as chairperson of its Church-State Committee.

This book is a collection of some previously published articles which are of continuing interest in the field of war, peace, and justice. His faculty colleagues, former students, and other friends have joined in publishing this book upon the occasion of his retirement from teaching and his designation as Professor Emeritus.

I

Pearl Harbor and Preparedness

(*Fellowship*, November, 1945)

In their campaign for supreme military power for the United States our officials have attempted to convince the people that armed might is the key to success in American diplomacy. Through concrete proposals to Congress and the people they have asked for peacetime military conscription, for many new naval bases, for a navy several times the size of any previous peacetime navy, for a standing army of 2,500,000[1] for a permanent armed reserve of at least four million men, for organized scientific research utilizing our best young scientists for military purposes, and for sole control of the atomic bomb. All this points in the direction of a super-military power beyond anything that pre-war Germany or Japan could boast.

The officials claim that such military might is essential to "adequate preparedness." And they are waging an intensive campaign to convince the public that we have been inadequately prepared in the past and therefore have either risked defeat or been forced to fight a long war.

The attack on Pearl Harbor and the defeat suffered there have been used by the President himself as illustrations of our lack of preparedness. The blame for Pearl Harbor he places on the American people because they did not want adequate preparedness. Army and Navy leaders, the American Legion, and some civilians also hold this view.

The Navy's Pearl Harbor report states that "On December 7, 1941, the United States (Pacific) Fleet was numerically inferior to the Japanese naval forces in both combatant and auxiliary vessels." Yet on the very day when Pearl Harbor was attacked, Secretary of Navy Knox issued a report stating that the United States Navy was the largest in the world. This means, of course, that a large part of our Navy was stationed in the Atlantic. This is explained in the Army's Pearl Harbor report: "The

---

[1] To be followed eventually by some reduction.

battle of the Atlantic was the predominant factor in the public mind and dominated the policy of the War Department, as evidenced by the transfer of a considerable part of the Pacific fleet to the Atlantic." The Army report also states that "much of our available military resources were being utilized to assist the United Nations."

Were We Prepared?

Actually, then the United States had the largest Navy in the world and was using perhaps half of it in "the battle of the Atlantic" at a time when the American people were led to believe we were not at war.

Moreover, the United States, in September, 1940, had established compulsory military training and service, as a result of which more than one million men were in the Army before Pearl Harbor was attacked. The Navy numbered over 600,000. The National Guard had been called to active service, and units of the Regular Army and Marine Corps were on duty throughout the Pacific.

So in addition to peacetime conscription the regular Army and the National Guard were fully mobilized for war.

The Army's Pearl Harbor report says: "Oahu (on which Pearl Harbor is situated) was also the location of one of the largest troop concentrations in the national defense system of the United States . . ." and "this outpost was implemented with the major portion of the fleet and very substantial Army installations in order that the mainland might rest securely and be protected."

General Marshall himself said in a letter to General Short, Commander of the Army's Hawaiian Department, on February 7, 1941, "Hawaii is on a far better basis than any other command in the Army." He also wrote, "Frankly I do not see any landing threat in the Hawaiian Island so long as *we have air superiority*."[2]

In the traditional "preparedness" sense, then Hawaii was the strongest post in the American defense setup.

Furthermore, a considerable part of the industrial might of the United States was already geared to war production and an even larger part of it was in the process of conversion to war production. If there was any lack of "preparedness" it was due to a decision on the part of those responsible for "preparedness" that we should give away not only 50 destroyers but also various kinds of military equipment to other nations. The Army's report stated, "We were arming our forces for war and at the same time giving away much of such armament."

The officials had decided not to let the American public know how quickly it was being taken into war. Ambassador Grew from Japan on September 30, 1941, "protested at the secrecy of our conversations with

---

[2] Italics supplied.

2

Japan as practised by the United States without advising the public, whereas it was common knowledge in Japan." The public, for example, was not told until the war was over just what sort of talk there had been behind the scenes about getting into war. Two illustrations[3] will suffice: "Mr. Hull said after delivering his ultimatum (on November 26, 1941) that he washed his hands of the matter and left it to the Army and Navy." In a letter to General Short, Chief of Staff Marshall said, "The United States desires that Japan commit the first overt act."

Thus, the United States was industrially as near to a war footing as possible without arousing the suspicions of the people. We were on enough of a war basis industrially to be supplying other nations with war materials.

Preparedness Incites Attack

In the light of these facts it is certainly not accurate to say that the United States was attacked because it was unprepared! Exactly the opposite is the case. The United States was attacked because our "preparedness" had reached such a point that Japan considered it a menace to her position in Asia. She decided to attack at once, before our armed forces became still more formidable. The Navy's Pearl Harbor report stresses this fact: "Aware of this existing weakness in relative fighting strength (of the Pacific fleet after units had been withdrawn to the Atlantic) and of the vigorous steps to overcome deficiencies, Japan early sensed the advantage of striking before these steps could become effective."

This observation by the Navy is practically an admission that an important factor in precipitating an attack is competition in armaments. Capt. B. H. Liddell Hart in his book *Why Don't We Learn From History?* says that an important factor in the beginning of the Second World War was Britain's adoption of peacetime conscription and an armaments program at the same time that she announced a military alliance with Poland and France. Capt. Liddell Hart even goes back to the First World War to show how imporant a factor great military power is in provoking attack. He points out that when a bill for conscription was introduced in Parliament prior to the war, the British General Staff advised against it on the grounds that it "would be a temptation to Germany to lose no time in launching a war. The General Staff expressed the view that, were they in the position of the great General Staff of Germany, they would strike at once." Capt. Hart states that Kuhlman, the former German Foreign minister, confirmed the surmise of the British General Staff.

---

[3] Both from the Pearl Harbor report.

[4] *Why Don't We Learn From History?* By Capt. B. H. Liddell Hart, Allen and Unwin, Ltd., London, England.

Did We Disarm Before?

Another piece of propaganda completely contrary to the facts has been used by American militarists in trying to sell a "preparedness" program. They say that "never again must the United States disarm." Thus they imply that the United States did disarm after other wars; but when Germany was disarmed following the First World War, we did not disarm. Though we did scrap some ships, in accordance with the famous 5:5:3 plan, we still maintained a large navy which, coupled with Britain's, was a controlling force in the world's oceans. Nor were France and England disarmed. M. Daladier testified at the Petain trial the "France was not disarmed" when Germany attacked. He said "France had 3,600 tanks against Germany's 3,200, and Germany's production was not greater than ours. After the armistice on June 24, 1940, there were 4,200 planes in the free zone." He did not add, as he might have, that France had had compulsory military service for years.

So far as Britain is concerned, we might recall Lloyd George's speech in the House of Commons (May 9, 1940) in which he said: "We gave, not merely in the treaty itself but in a document signed by M. Clemenceau (then Premier of France) on our behalf, a solemn promise that if Germany disarmed we would immediately follow her example. That was not carried out and there is no government more responsible for that than the present (British) National Government which came to power in 1931 . . . America was ready. Germany was ready. Bruening (Chancellor of Germany) was in charge. We refused to carry out our promise, for Germany was completely disarmed."

Does Preparedness Aid Diplomacy?

Still another argument advanced in favor of a big military program is that a nation with a large military establishment can more effectively win diplomatic victories in its relations with other nations. General Marshall, Chief of Staff of the United States Army, said, in speaking of peacetime compulsory military training, "The officials of the State Department have been strongly of the opinion that a decision in this matter prior to the final peace negotiations would greatly strengthen the hand of the United States in securing acceptance of a genuine organization to handle international difference."

Yet, at the very moment when the United States was the sole possessor of the atomic bomb, the owner of a navy larger than all other navies combined, and had several million soldiers in Europe, our diplomats were unable to prevent Russia from extending her diplomatic and military control over the Balkans, and the foreign ministers of Russia, Britain, and the United States were unable to arrive at any agreement about a peace treaty for Italy or joint control of Japan! If military

4

preparedness really gains diplomatic victories, how can we account for this conspicuous failure?

International discussions conducted in the atmosphere of threats and fear are unlikely to solve the world's problems, but are likely to result in the development of spheres of influence and international distrust. The fact is, military preparedness can be effective in diplomacy only if the nation using it is willing to go to war. But in that case such destructive forces are unleashed that even if military victory is achieved, genuine victory for democracy is likely to be lost.

Preparedness or Peace?

The truth about military preparedness, of which Pearl Harbor is but another striking illustration, may be set down and underscored as follows:

First, great military power does not provide real security. A daring and well executed surprise attack by the enemy, or a miscalculation by the President or other key officials in Washington, may almost totally offset the advantage of "adequate preparedness" in munitions plants, fortifications, ground forces, and naval vessels. The atomic bomb greatly increases this danger. We cannot rule out the possibility that even a small nation, with a few hundred planes each dropping one or more atomic bombs, might put the United States Navy, all its island bases, and the key munitions and military centers on the mainland out of commission in less than twenty-four hours.

Second, war preparations and peace preparations are incompatible. They cannot be effectively combined. Either we believe in nationalism, or we believe in world organization; we believe in diplomacy backed by force, or we believe in diplomacy backed by friendship. There is no middle ground. So long as the world prepares for war we shall have Secretaries of State issuing ultimatums and handing the matter over to the Army and Navy to settle — and we shall have in the hands of aggressor nations the power to carry out their aggression.

What the world needs is American leadership in the direction of genuine world organization and complete disarmament. Yet at this particular moment in history our government is working as never before to make the United States the supreme military power of all time.

II

The Failure of Conscription in Europe

(Motive, March, 1949)

> The traditional militaryism of Europe, as tested over and over by history, has afforded no more than a cream-puff security. If we look at the evidence, we must admit the failure of this system is no accident.

When war began in Europe on September 1, 1939, there seemed little doubt of the outcome. Germany had rearmed and had reinstituted conscription less than five years before. France and Poland, on the other hand, had seasoned armies, a long history of peacetime conscription, and plans for immediate mobilization. A survey of European and American opinion, both civilian and military, shows just how much faith was placed in the program of peacetime military training.

French military leaders were confident that the Maginot Line and universal military training made invasion of France impossible. Their argument, summed up in the book *Is Invasion Still Possible?* was based on the assumption that millions of trained men, ready for immediate mobilization, either would serve as a deterrent to invasion or actually would prevent it.

Likewise the Polish premier, General Felicjan Slawoj Skladkowski, on September 2, 1939, told a joint session of Parliament that "the unconquerable Polish army will defeat its historic enemy."

The Knoxville, Tennessee, *News Sentinel,* of September 1, 1939, quoted a dispatch from Warsaw which said, "Every able-bodied man in Poland between the ages of eighteen and forty is under arms. Poland has an army of four million and although it has less armaments than Germany, it has more men in the field, and there are plenty of rifles and bullets for all . . . and there are millions more men beyond forty capable and willing to fight." Poland had had peacetime conscription, and every one of her millions of men had had at least a year of compulsory military training.

American military leaders and writers, who had long favored compulsory military training in the United States, were equally emphatic in their belief that Germany could not defeat France and Poland. Major George Fielding Eliot and Major R. Ernest Dupuy, field artillery, U.S. Army, wrote in 1937 in their book, *If War Comes*, of the "tactical and technical factors favoring France so far as material and training are concerned." Of Germany they wrote: "Despite the strenuous and efficient military schools now in full swing, the hiatus in military training imposed by the Versailles Treaty is too severe a handicap to be overcome in a short time."

The Baltimore *Sun*, of September 10, 1939, reported an interview with "officers of the general staff, Third Corps Area" of the U. S. Army. The officers felt that the Polish retreat left "plenty of hope" that the well-trained Polish army would "stem the drive of German mechanized forces."

A New York *Times* correspondent writing from Paris on September third stated that "the Germans have lost any initial advantage conditioned on surprise. Their opponents are fully prepared." Earlier the *Times* (September 2, 1939) had quoted the Associated Press as saying "the French land army could be raised to eight million well-trained, well-equipped men" whose "places in the giant military machine have been determined long since." When the French mobilized, they did so "calmly and efficiently," according to a report in the New York *Herald Tribune* of September third. The report added, "The machinery which has been prepared through the years from November 11, 1918, worked smoothly." The New York *Herald Tribune* of September 4, 1939, under a Paris September third dateline, reported, "Premier Edouard Daladier led France into war tonight with his people confident of victory. For twenty years they have prepared for this struggle, done their service in the army, navy or air force, spent billions of francs for guns and munitions. This time they believe they are ready."

Major George Field Eliot in his September 3, 1939, column in the New York *Herald Tribune* wrote that "Left alone, Germany could probably defeat Poland in the end, though probably not as quickly as some boasts have suggested. But there is no doubt whatever that it is impossible for Germany to defeat Poland, plus Britain. I cannot emphasize this too strongly. If Germany is confronted with Poland, France and Britain in arms, Germany is most assuredly going to be defeated."

Despite this confidence in sheer numbers, Germany did defeat Poland and France, as well as the British armies which had crossed the channel. An American newspaper correspondent writing in the Baltimore *Sun*, of September 14, 1939, summed up the situation in a description of the destruction of Poland. He said: "It has brought its lessons, this lightning war which so many believed impossible in a Europe so armed and ready." It is significant that those European leaders who followed the misleading advice to "prepare for war if you want peace" had the almost unanimous approval of military writers and army leaders in America. Even today, although the lessons of history are clear, the American press, including its military analysts and the army leadership, continues to accept the same philosophy and advocates essentially the same universal training program.

If we look at the record of the last war, we discover that a small, largely volunteer German army drove into Poland so rapidly that eight days after the invasion Germany had occupied one fifth of the entire area of the country. (Chicago *Tribune,* September 8, 1939.) In the First World War, it had taken nine months to occupy the same territory. The German drives into Poland were led by German tanks "in squadrons of 120, 240 and sometimes even 450 smashing along in formation." (New York *Times* September 6, 1939.)

In commenting on the invasion of Poland, an AP correspondent writing from Poland on September thirteenth about the Polish mass armies, asked, "Why has the Polish army, although so large in numbers, been thrown back?"

Despite the faith of many Americans in the European system of military conscription, it was no answer to lightning war. The New York *Times,* of September 24, 1939, carried a news dispatch which stated, "Last Wendesday, twenty days after the German juggernaut began to roll over Poland, General Colonel Walther von Brauchitsch, commander-in-chief of the German army, issued this order of the day: 'Soldiers! the great battle in the Vistula sector is finished. The Polish army is annihilated. The operations against Poland are thus concluded.'" William L. Shirer in his *Berlin Diary* wrote that "at the end of eighteen days of fighting, not a single Polish division, not even a brigade, was left intact." Yet these men had had more military training than is proposed by our army under the universal military training program.

Nor was Poland without allies when she went down to defeat. A September 3, 1939, Paris dispatch in the Baltimore *Sun,* of September fourth, stated "France joined Great Britain in war against Germany today and eight million Frenchmen moved toward the front."

When the German army turned its attention to the conscript armies of Western Europe, it knocked out Denmark in one day and shortly thereafter Norway had been occupied. The invasion began on the ninth of April, and on April 24, 1940, "Germany took over direct control of Norway." On May ninth, Germany invaded Belgium, Luxembourg and the Netherlands. On the fifteenth, the Netherlands army capitulated. On the twenty-eighth the Belgian army surrendered, and two days later Britain began evacuating Dunkirk. Shirer's *Berlin Diary* commented on May fourteenth, "We're all a little dazed tonight by the news. The Dutch army has capitulated — after only five days of fighting. What happened . . . to its army of over half a million men?"

The Pittsburgh *Press,* of May 28, 1940, stated: "In eighteen days the Third Reich has crushed Belgium and Holland and the best forces France and England could send . . ."

By June 14, 1940, the French army based on a system of universal military training in peacetime which from 1935 had demanded two years' military training and service was in dire straits. On that day, France appealed to the United States for help, stating: "Our divisions are decimated. Generals are commanding battalions." Three days later, on June seventeenth, France asked armistice terms of Germany. Marshal Petain was suing for "peace with honor."

Universal military training did not prevent war, and it did not prevent defeat. Yet the heroes of the victorious French in World War I, Foch, Petain, Gamelin, Maginot, had insisted upon peacetime conscription as a prerequisite to future peace for France.

Dr. A. Allan Bates, an American scientist who spent years in France, explained to a Congressional committee the principles on which opposition to UMT on the part of some scientists and engineers in France is based. He added: "However, with the aid of a continuous newspaper campaign and backed by the dead weight of overwhelming tradition, the prestige of the general staff triumphed. France put her billions of francs and her millions of boy-years into universal military training."

If we turn to the East, we discover that the Japanese conscript armies, like those of Europe, were of little use. When Japan agreed to unconditional surrender, her home army of almost four million men had never fired a shot nor even seen an American soldier.

Only the untested Swiss and Swedish systems of peacetime conscription have been referred to as "successful" by American army spokesmen. A few military men have admitted that economic, strategic and topographical reasons were responsible for Swiss and Swedish neutrality, but many of our "military experts" are so wedded to the concept of conscription that they attribute Swiss neutrality to Germany's fear of Swiss riflemen.

The failure of peacetime conscription in Europe and Asia was the failure of a system, and not just an accident. A well-developed military bureaucracy, the regimentation of the boyhood of a nation during the formative period of their lives, the belief that important problems can be solved by military methods or can be avoided by the threat of adequate military force, are results of the conscription system. On the basis of the evidence we have, there is no reason to believe that conscription will serve America better than it served Europe.

III

The Growing Power
of The Military

(*The Progressive*, January, 1959)

One of the foundations of democratic government is freedom from military domination. In a democratic society the military is simply one branch of the executive with no authority or duty other than that of defending the nation's interests against external enemies. This principle has been carefully observed by every American generation until our own.

Today in America the military has achieved such power in government, business, education, public opinion, and other key areas of our national life as to endanger the very basis of our democracy. We have come perilously close to turning America into a garrison state, a state in which public opinion is so security-conscious that military leadership is welcomed in the civil service, military budgets dominate the economy, military considerations largely determine foreign policy, and the officer corps expands its influence even into the voluntary associations of citizens.

We have moved so far in this direction that warnings from public officials are received with little or no concern by their fellow citizens or their fellows in Congress. There was, for example, scarcely a ripple over this protest by Senator Ralph E. Flanders, Vermont Republican, on the Senate floor:

"It is not only that we are sacrificing to defense our standard of living and the free independence or our economic life. We are sacrificing our freedom itself. We are being forced to shift the American way of life into the pattern of the garrison state."

Fifty years ago such warnings would not have gone unheeded. Then the American Army was small and clearly under civilian control. Even by 1920, after America's first world-wide military experience, the total personnel of the Army, the Navy, and the Marines was only 354,366. By the end of 1957 the Regular Armed Forces totaled 2,794,883 and the military establishment was definitely in the saddle. In addition to the uniformed force, there were 1,348,766 civilian employees of the defense department, well over half of the civilian staff of the federal government. If we add the paid and unpaid reserves of 3,468,358, the total of those with a vested interest in the military establishment approximate 7,500,000.

The civilian and military personnel administer a yearly appropriation of more than $45 billion, roughly two-thirds of the total federal budget for 1959.

The Cordiner Report to the Secretary of Defense valued the property of the Defense Department at $160 billion, "by any yardstick of measurement the world's largest organization." Is it small wonder that the Defense Department, the world's largest organization, should dwarf the rest of the United States government both in size and in influence?

In the United States alone the Pentagon owns more than 32 million acres of land and in foreign countries an additional 2.6 million acres. The total acreage is greater than the areas of Rhode Island, Delaware, Connecticut, New Jersey, Massachusetts, Vermont, New Hampshire, and Maryland combined.

The activities of the Defense Department, said the Cordiner Report, "are spread throughout the 48 states and are located in 16,000 cities. They are conducted abroad in 52 foreign countries." This widespread operation gives the Pentagon wide influence in domestic and foreign policy. For some years the military has dominated our foreign policy, though rarely does a public official acknowledge this usurpation as boldly as did A. A. Ribicoff, then a key member of the House Foreign Affairs Committee, in 1952, "In my opinion," Ribicoff, now Governor of Connecticut, said, "in the last year or two more foreign policy has been made in the Pentagon than in the State Department."

The fact that this influence has not declined since 1952 is evident from the way in which Admiral Lewis Strauss, until recently of the AEC, Admiral Radford, formerly head of the Joint Chiefs of Staff, and others in the Pentagon, with the assistance of Secretary of State Dulles, were able to scuttle Harold Stassen's efforts to negotiate a disarmament agreement with the Russians in 1957 — in spite of the fact that President Eisenhower and the head of the Policy Planning Division of the State Department had given their approval to Stassen's proposal.

The economic power of the Pentagon reaches into every corner of the nation. Military assets, for example, are three times as great as the combined assets of United States Steel, American Telephone and Telegraph, Metropolitan Life Insurance, General Motors, and Standard Oil of New Jersey. Similarly, the Defense Department's paid personnel total is about three times the number of all the employees of these companies. But this is only part of the story, for many of the largest civilian industries are themselves directly or indirectly receiving funds from the Pentagon. Between 85 and 90 percent of the aircraft industry's production in 1955, for example, went to the armed forces.

The big companies with scarcely an exception hire many retired generals and admirals either as consultants or vice presidents. These officers who are well paid by the companies, in addition to their retirement pay ranging from $6,000 to $19,531 a year, provide a liaison between the big corporations and the Pentagon. That this is a profitable business practice may be deduced from Senator Paul Douglas's revelation in the Senate, July 1, 1957, that 92 percent of military contracts were negotiated without competitive bidding.

Military leaders are actively engaged in drafting and promoting legislation; they have an extensive propaganda network that makes carefully planned use of the press, Hollywood, radio, television, and other media; they share in the preparation of the national budget; and in various ways they exercise an influence in civilian organizations.

All this was accomplished before the White House was occupied by the three generals: Dwight D. Eisenhower as President, General Wilton B. Persons as Assistant to the President, and Brigadier General Andrew J. Goodpaster as White House Staff Secretary. The process has simply been accelerated since the White House was taken over.

The story of this drive for military control begins more than 40 years ago, during World War I. The Army's General Staff prepared a bill which would have increased its power and provided for a large standing army and compulsory military training for teen-age boys. Congress rejected compulsory military training and whittled down the requested size of the standing army in passing the National Defense Act of 1920, but elements in the Army, working with Congressional opponents of President Wilson, succeeded in limiting the authority of the civilian Secretary of War over the Army. Army officers were, in effect, permitted to go over the head of their civilian superior to present their position directly to Congressional committees.

Instead of curbing the Army or Navy, members of Congressional committees on military affairs developed a vested interest in expansion of the armed forces. This has gone so far that today, under Representative Carl Vinson's firm control, the House Armed Service Committee is practically the alter ego of the Pentagon. Vinson stated his philosophy in the House, March 30, 1949, when he asserted that the President's decision "is not the expert military view. Our top source for military judgment is the Joint Chiefs of Staff . . ." So fully does he believe this that he gives priority to the Pentagon over civilian groups of government charged with over-all economic or budgetary planning. "And as between the Bureau of the Budget and the Joint Chiefs of Staff," he said, "I will place my confidence in the latter, in regard to what our national defense needs are." This attitude of ratification of military desires is precisely what the Pentagon wants and cultivates.

Another World War I development was the National Defense Act of 1916 which authorized the War Department to establish R.O.T.C. units in schools and colleges. Shortly thereafter the War Department, without any legal right, began its pressure on land grant colleges to make military training compulsory for all first and second year students.

In spite of these military gains the Army remained relatively small, having only 138,569 men and a budget of $273,421,902 in 1935. In 1941 the Army jumped to 1.4 million men from 267,767 the previous year. Writing of these pre-war years, Donald Nelson, the prominent business executive who headed the War Production Board, said in his *Arsenal of Democracy* that the Army felt itself "starved and ignored." By the close of World War II, however, Nelson was fearful of Army power. The war had brought an opportunity for increased military influence. Nelson pointed out that "from 1982 onward the Army people, in order to get control of our national economy, did their best to make an errand boy of the WPB."

A Bureau of the Budget report, *The United States at War*, published in 1946, said that during World War II the Army sought "total control of the nation, its manpower, its facilities, its economy." When a particular effort to seize control was frustrated by the President or by Donald Nelson "the military leaders took another approach to secure the same result; they never abandoned the sincere conviction that they could run things better and more expeditiously than the civilians."

Unfortunately, a combination of Congressional willingness to let military men run the war and a tendency of President Roosevelt to deal directly with the Joint Chiefs of Staff resulted in a weakening of civilian control. The Secretaries of War and Navy were not only excluded from important strategy matters, but were not even put on the routine distribution list for the papers of the Joint Chiefs of Staff. Roosevelt also excluded the State Department, so that it had only a peripheral role even in matters that might determine postwar foreign policy. The Joint Chiefs became so accustomed to power and to formulating major policy that they were unable to accept with good grace being overruled.

Donald Nelson, concerned with this lust for power, warned in the concluding section of his book that "the question of military control will confront us not only in war but in peace. The lesson taught by these recent war years is clear: our whole economic and social system will be in peril if it is controlled by the military men."

When the war ended, the military took advantage of the unsettled condition of the world to consolidate its power. Charles E. Wilson, president of General Electric, had pointed the way by suggesting both an alliance of big business and the military, and "a permanent war economy." In an address to the Army Ordnance Association in January, 1944, he warned that "the revulsion against war not too long hence will be an almost insuperable obstacle for us to overcome in establishing a preparedness program and for that reason I am convinced that we must begin now to set the machinery in motion." Wilson went on to suggest that every big company appoint a special executive to act as liaison man with the armed forces, with the commission of a colonel in the reserve. He added:

"First of all such a program must be the responsibility of the federal government. It must be initiated and administered by the executive branch — by the President as Commander-in-Chief and by the War and Navy Departments. Of equal importance is the fact that this must be, once and for all, a continuing program and not the creature of an emergency. In fact one of its objects will be to eliminate emergencies so far as possible. The role of Congress is limited to voting the needed funds. Industry's role in this program is to respond and cooperate . . . in the execution of the part allotted to it; industry must not be hampered by political witch-hunts, or thrown to the fanatical isolationist fringe tagged with a 'merchants of death' label."

As a result of this reasoning and the need to appease its own insatiable appetite, the military entered a marriage of convenience with big business. Both have faithfully performed their vows, the Pentagon creating a climate of fear of war and industry responding profitably with the weapons. So firm has military control become that "the role of Congress" has indeed been "limited to voting the needed funds."

Colonel William Neblett, who for years was stationed in the Pentagon, asserted in 1953 in his book *Pentagon Politics*, that the Pentagon planned a nationwide campaign to create the impression "that we were living in a state of undeclared emergency, that war with Russia was just around the corner," and that a large military establishment with all the trappings would be essential in the foreseeable future. So effective was the military's program and so clear the evidence of Communist expansion that many civilians who normally would have insisted on a different course were prepared to let our strategy for dealing with communism be dominated by military considerations.

In this atmosphere at least seven steps were taken by the Pentagon leadership. The first step was to eliminate civilian control over the armed forces by establishing a supreme General Staff nominally under civilian control but, as James Forrestal charged, "in actual practice and result really in the hands of one military Chief of Staff."

General George Marshall, who was the moving spirit behind most

14

of the early efforts to expand military control, proposed "a Chief of Staff to the President, to serve the President in exercising his functions as constitutional Commander-in-Chief of the Armed Forces." In practice this meant a military officer with immediate access to the President, and, in effect, functioning for the President on military matters. Marshall defined this job as serving the President on all "matters relating to strategy, tactics and operation, preparation and presentation of the joint military budget and on such other matters as he may consider pertinent to his constitutional function as Commander-in-Chief . . ." When this proposal was not adopted, the Army took other steps to expand military influence over civil government.

The next step was the transfer of military officers to key posts in civilian departments of government, especially in the State Department. The Washington *Star* reported February 2, 1947, that "Ten of the 20 men ranking as executive officers in the State Department have been brought in during recent months from the military services." A few months later the New York *Times* revealed that when General John H. Hilldring was made an Assistant Secretary of State, "he brought with him to the State Department 26 of his assistants in the War Department."

That the Army was conscious of its new power was evident in a paragraph in the January 18, 1947, *Army and Navy Bulletin* which began with these words: "Today the Army has virtual control of foreign affairs . . ."

In 1953 there were nine Army generals and 58 colonels assigned to civilian agencies of government. The number would be much greater if retired officers were included, to say nothing of Air Force and Navy personnel. By 1957 about 200 generals or admirals were on assignment to other departments of government, international or interservice agencies, more than 1,300 colonels or naval personnel of comparable rank, and about 6,000 officers of lower grade.

A few Senators and Congressmen protested this development but Congress as a whole acquiesced. The chairman of the Senate Committee on Post Office and Civil Service, William Langer, told the Senate in June, 1948, about "military men who were taken out of the army by the high military authorities and placed in the civil service of the United States where we cannot get rid of them without changing our entire civil service structure."

Representatives R. J. Twyman of Illinois, Robert H Mollohan of West Virginia, and Lee Metcalf of Montana were among a number of other members of Congress who protested the military infiltration of civilian jobs. Twyman in 1948 lamented the fact that the President "has seen fit to staff the traditionally civilian positions of government, particularly in the diplomatic and consular service, with retired Army and Navy officers."

Lee Metcalf in March, 1956, tried to stop the mounting control by military men. He said: "Already we have a general in the first echelon of the Immigration and Naturalization Service. Already we have a general in the second echelon. It seems to me that civilians should show up in here somewhere." Metcalf's effort failed, and the normally civilian Immigration and Naturalization Service passed completely over to military control.

Since the armed forces are as concerned with influencing Congress as they are the Administration, an effective military lobby composed of "liaison officers" with Congress has been developed. In addition, military officers have office space in and function in the House and Senate office buildings "assisting" some Congressional committees.

A third development was the long campaign for universal military training from 1944 through 1955. General Marshall had decided the Army would not take "no" from Congress. His successors pursued the same policy because the officer corps wanted a large, permanently guaranteed force for them to command. It also wanted UMT in order to indoctrinate young America in militarism. Assistant Secretary of Defense Anna Rosenberg said in 1952, "A large part of the training as envisaged . . . by the Department of Defense is citizenship training, literary training, training in morale and training in the type of things that young people ought to have." The Pentagon feared civilian schools would not give the right slant to citizenship training.

Colonel Neblett wrote that "when the bill did not pass, the Pentagon was thrown into complete confusion." The generals simply did not dream that Congress would defy them. General Ira Eaker spoke of the "appallingly bad judgment" of the "Old men" in Congress "who would have been eliminated in any other nation."

"The Pentagon," wrote Colonel Neblett, "turned on the heat. The huge professional officers' corps was converted into a propaganda organization, the like of which the world had never seen. Generals and admirals, colonels, and captains, spoke throughout the land at every meeting to which they could wrangle an invitation." It was only the combined efforts of church, farm, labor, and educational groups that stiffened Congressional resistance. Although defeated on UMT, the military succeeded in 1951 in making the Selective Service System a permanent institution and in 1955 in getting compulsory reserve legislation adopted solely to establish the principle of universal conscription.

A fourth development was the National Security Act of 1947, through which the military establishment gained a formal voice in determining foreign and domestic policy. Whether by design or accident the public debate on the NSA revolved almost entirely around the issue of unification of the armed forces. Yet the most important feature of the bill provides for a National Security Council to advise the President on the integration of domestic, foreign, and military policies relating to national security. In addition to the Secretary of Defense, who is legally a member, the chairman of the Joint Chiefs of Staff, not a member by law, has regularly attended meetings.

Since Council decisions are not published, it is impossible for the American people to challenge the thinking that produces these far-reaching decisions. It is known, however, that when the military agencies and the State Department representatives disagree, the President makes the final decision. And in May, 1951, in answer to a question from Senator Styles Bridges on this point, General Marshall replied: "I can recall no occasion when Mr. Truman has acted adversely to the Chiefs of Staff and the Secretary of Defense in relation to the State Department."

A fifth step was the organization of a tremendous public relations program whose purpose is to build a climate friendly to the military and also sell the current military program to the people. In 1950, military public relations received an appropriation of more than 9.5 million dollars. It was increased in 1951 to more than 12 million.

These millions are greatly augmented through the Pentagon policy of persuading business firms as well as radio and TV networks to donate "publicity." *Variety* has estimated that an additional $6,000,000 is what the various military shows would cost on a radio time-and-talent basis. the networks and advertising agencies write off their contributions as "public service," except for agency executive expense accounts which the government foots.

Still another illustration of the tremendous public relations activity of the military establishment is the work of the Pictorial Branch. In one year this branch helped private motion pictures develop movies favorable to the Army which "would add up to about $30 million" of free publicity, according to a Defense Department spokesman. In describing this work he said: "The impression they convey must be a correct one because much of the attitude of the public toward the Army, Navy, and Air Force . . . revolves around these pictures which have a very great influence on the public. It is stuff that we simply couldn't buy, and it is priceless."

The Pentagon's propaganda machine is divided into sections such as the Press Department, which sees that a military press conference is held every morning and afternoon so as to get into morning and afternoon papers. There is a magazine and book branch which prepares material for magazine articles and books. The director of Pentagon publicity in 1953 cited the *Saturday Evening Post* which "in the last year carried 57 articles" on military subjects, as one indication of its success.

Even these do not cover the amazing number of propaganda activities. The Army owns the largest motion picture studio in the East. It has a speakers' bureau and turns out speeches for officers and reserve officers to deliver. It sends exhibits to county and state fairs and to national conventions and universities. It has a Special Events Branch which arranges parades and other military observances across the nation.

One of the most important of the Pentagon propaganda activities is pushed by the National Organization Branch, through which officers cultivate officials of national civilian organizations to influence them to support the military line. This branch, for example, persuades national organizations to invite a general or admiral to speak at the organization's national convention.

A sixth step in the expansion of military influence has been a large-scale invasion of the field of education. The present pattern of military financing of academic research was begun in World War II. Financial returns and prestige were big factors in university decisions to continue accepting military contracts after the war had ended. In 1947, the Army earmarked $70,000,000 for basic studies in colleges. In 1948-49, the office of Naval Research spent approximately $20,000,000 on about 500 projects in more than 150 colleges and universities. By 1956, the federal government was spending annually about $150 million for scientific research in colleges and universities, and another $150 million was granted to universities for the operation of large government owned enterprises such as the Los Alamos and Argonne Laboratories. Most of these funds are administered by the Department of Defense and the Atomic Energy Commission.

There was also an expansion of military training units on college campuses in the post-war years. The Navy succeeded in getting the Holloway Plan made law, permitting it to pay the full tuition, fees, books, laboratory expenses and an additional retainer of $600 a year to Naval R.O.T.C. students in 52 colleges and universities.

By 1952 more than 300,000 students or about one-fourth of the male college population were in Army, Navy, or Air Force R.O.T.C. units. The expected R.O.T.C. enrollment for 1959 is 312,852 students at a cost of $30,798,000. In about half of the colleges R.O.T.C. is compulsory for the first two years of student life.

As a producer of officers, R.O.T.C. is wasteful and inefficient, since 73 percent of them quit as soon as their required service is over. Actually the armed forces use R.O.T.C. for indoctrination and propaganda purposes. "They want uniformity throughout the whole R.O.T.C. system," wrote Walter Millis. "They believe that the purpose of the R.O.T.C. teaching should be to indoctrinate and inspire rather than to inculcate that capacity for critical understanding which is the presumed object of a civilian educational system."

Wherever the military finds an opportunity, it moves into other areas of our national life. Even the Boy Scouts have not been overlooked. The 1945 annual report of the Boy Scouts of America revealed an agreement with the Air Force "whereby 12 liaison officers have been designated by the Army Air Force to cooperate in making more effective the Air Scout program . . ." The "request for this agreement," said the June-July, 1956, magazine *Scouting*, "came from the commanding general of the Army Air Forces." The Air Force later stated in an official report: "The U.S. Air Force will continue to support the Air Scout program for its public relations and public education values and although the existing agreement between this headquarters precludes the active use of the Air Scout movement as a personnel procurement source it is recognized that the program presents an admirable medium for the dissemination of the missions, objectives, and problems of the USAF to a widespread and receptive public audience."

So thorough has been the military penetration of civilian government and civilian life that it could hardly have been accomplished without some careful planning. And so thoroughly has the civilian mind accepted this military culture that there is little organized protest. This would have been unthinkable 50 years ago or even 20 years ago.

The danger to our people and to the world of this militarization of our society is great. The military mind, as Drew Middleton of the New York *Times* once observed, has an attitude of "conformity" in the "daily routines" that tends "to extend to thought processes as well." It has a "dislike of some of the less efficient methods of getting things done that are a part of our political process."

But the greatest danger is that we permit military considerations to guide our relations with other nations. The tendency of generals and admirals to be tough, with a guided missile or an atom bomb as the big stick of the space age, needs to be curbed and eliminated, or we shall again and again be led to the very threshold of war, for concentration of power in military hands is always regarded as a provocation and threat to other nations.

It is hardly necessary to point out that the vast expansion of the American military machine cannot be stopped or the trend reversed without a major revolution in our foreign policy as well as in our whole culture. But this is not impossible if we begin to think for ourselves and organize for the democratic replacement of military domination by civilian authority. Democracy can flourish only if it is practiced. No people can turn the important decisions of life over to its army without eventually becoming controlled by that army.

IV

Taproot of Militarism

(Engage, May 15, 1971)

Ten Myths Used in Defense of the Draft

Conscription, as we have known it, beginning with Napoleon, was intended to produce mass armies cheaply so as to gain or hold territory. It has been understood to be the "taproot of militarism" for two reasons. It gave the top professionals or officers virtually unlimited access to young men so as to indoctrinate and use them as they desired. It also compelled young men to enter the military and thus abandon their normal civil liberties.

The degree to which our society has been militarized is evident in the fallacious myths set forth in defense of conscription and still believed by otherwise rational people.

Myth one: "If the draft ends, the United States will not be able to maintain large overseas garrisons and therefore we shall return to isolationism." The opposite of isolationism is not imperialism, evident in control of land by overseas garrisons. It is world cooperation, evident in international organization such as the United Nations and in conferences seeking disarmament. Militarists confuse national military expansion overseas with internationalism.

Myth two: "If the draft ends, we shall have a career or professional military." The Air Force, the Navy, most of the Marine Corps and a part of the Army have been and are volunteers. More than two-thirds of the armed forces are true (not draft-induced) volunteers. The officers who make the decisions are all volunteers. The method of original enlistment, whether by draft or volunteering, does not determine professionalism. A career army is built by long-term re-enlistments and could only be prevented by prohibiting all re-enlistments. Militarists confuse the initial method of voluntary enlistment with a career or professional army in order to argue for a draft.

Myth three: "Ending the draft means reliance on mercenaries." The term *mercenaries* refers to foreign paid troops. All American military men receive pay and presumably have more reasons than money for entering the armed forces. The U.S. has used more mercenaries in the Vietnam war than in any previous war, while using large numbers of U.S. draftees. There is no necessary relation of mercenaries either to a draft or a voluntary force, but militarists persist in their claims.

Myth four: "Volunteers won't fight in unpopular wars. Therefore the draft is needed." Once a man is in the armed forces he must obey orders whether he is a volunteer or a conscript. A contract, voluntarily entered, does not give a choice of non-performance. Volunteers in the Green Berets, Marines, and Air Force fought in Vietnam as well as drafted soldiers.

Myth five: "The draft is largely responsible for the unpopularity of the war in Vietnam, because families with draftees or those about to be drafted have been the chief opponents of the war." Many of the chief opponents and demonstrators in the streets were students with deferments, theological students, clergy, etc., who were not vulnerable to the draft. It is significant that with the ending of student deferments there have been fewer demonstrations, but this appears to have no cause-effect relationship.

Myth six: "The draft will civilianize the army or at least diffuse professional military influence." On the contrary, the Army drills and indoctrinates civilians. Is the all-volunteer Navy or Air Force more militaristic than the Army? In all three branches new recruits enter monthly from civilian life. There is no evidence that drafted men disobey orders more often or act more humanely toward Vietnamese villagers than first-term volunteers who have received the same military training. Is one son who volunteers more likely to be militarized than his brother who is drafted? Civilian control of the military must be in the hands of full-time civilians, not former civilians under the command of their officers.

Myth seven: "Responsibility to society or to country requires forced military service." This assumes that non-military contributions to society are not as significant as military ones. It also assumes that a free society can be maintained or served best by depriving some members of society of their freedom. Forcing people to do what the government decides regardless of their values and abilities is the essence of totalitarianism rather than democracy.

Myth eight: Pay adequate to induce volunteering will result in an army composed of the poor." The very poor who cannot qualify physically because of poor nutrition and little medical care during childhood are not acceptable under either the draft or the higher volunteer standards. The President's Commission on an All-Volunteer Armed Forces said, "Our research indicates that an all-volunteer force will not differ sig-

21

nificantly from the current force of conscripts and volunteers." The Department of Defense figures (see below) on educational level reveal how many volunteers came from those able to afford college and able to continue through high school without dropping out to work or because of disabilities associated with poverty or minority frustration.

Table on Education Prior to Military Service
(figures represent thousands)

Those born in 1938 who entered military service

| | Number of School Years Completed | | |
	12 yrs.	13-15 yrs.	16+ yrs.
Volunteer	191.2	36.9	5.2
Draftees	35.6	17.1	5.5
Officers	0.1	1.3	35.9

Those born in 1947 who entered military service

	12 yrs.	13-15 yrs.	16+ yrs.
Volunteer	230.8	44.1	5.3
Draftees	21.9	10.5	3.4
Officers	.2	1.2	34.3

Myth nine: "Adequate pay will lead to an all black or largely black army." Since most blacks are living near or below the poverty level, the same response can be made as was to an "army of the poor." The President's Commission on an All-Volunteer Armed Force said, "Blacks who join a voluntary force presumably have decided for themselves that military service is preferable to the other alternatives available to them . . . Denial of this opportunity would reflect either bias or a paternalistic belief that blacks are not capable of making the 'right' decisions concerning their lives."

Myth ten: "The draft is more equitable and hence more democratic than a voluntary system." This assumes that the equality of involuntary servitude rather than freedom is the essence of democracy. Equal treatment under compulsion, even if it could be achieved, is not the basis for or evidence of a free society. Those who foster this myth hope we will think of equitability or even equality among those forced to serve. Instead those forced into the Army are exploited by the more powerful adults and treated as powerless second-class citizens. The draft is pushed principally by wealthy men in the military-industrial complex, by well to-do politicians, and by well-paid Generals. As John Galbraith put it, "The draft survives principally as a device by which we use compulsion to get young men to serve at less than the market rate of pay."

22

The conscript is taxed the difference between the military pay he gets and the rate of pay that would induce him to volunteer. A man who would be induced by $4,500 a year to enlist, but receives only $2,000 as a draftee, pays an annual tax of $2,500. If he were drafted out of, or prevented from accepting, a civilian job paying $6,000 a year, his tax would be $4,000.

In addition to these ten myths designed to perpetuate the military draft, there is a current proposal for labor conscription, deceptively called "national service." It is intended as a device to force all teen-agers either into the military or into some alternate form of government work such as education, conservation land and water reclamation, or social service in depressed or ghetto areas. The assumptions behind it are the same as those of totalitarian philosophers, that everyone is obligated to work for the state, that collective or group discipline is to be fostered by the state, that since we owe so much to the state we, or in this case powerless youth, should work at little or no pay.

A free society is based on the assumption that the state exists to serve its citizens, that there is nothing dishonorable about being paid for work, that a man fulfills his obligation to society not in a period of compulsory service but through his life long vocation and his voluntary participation in civic organizations.

National service is nationalist rather than internationalist in its orientation. It assumes that the nation-state may do what is constitutionally forbidden to private employers — place persons into involuntary servitude. Millions of people who are unemployed or under-employed could be induced by adequate wages to work in goverment-sponsored projects. Instead, those who want national service prefer to compel those who are employed, or preparing for their vocations, to work at jobs they otherwise would not have chosen.

Some proposals for national service are modeled on the kind of alternate service required of conscientious objectors. They are drafted but assigned to work for approved employers or organizations. Should the state through national service assign drafted youth to work in churches or hospitals, or should we assume that voluntary work for a church or hospital serves society better? What happens if a church or other organization is not approved by the national service agency? Is it the business of government to approve voluntary organizations?

Our society has millions of young people in colleges preparing for a lifetime of service or at work building roads, teaching school, or farming, etc. If there has been any erosion among other youth of the idea of competent voluntary service in our society, perhaps we should ask whether the long-continued peacetime draft is the reason. The draft has been the basis also for what General Hershey called "channelling" of young men into jobs deemed to be in the national interest.

"Channelling" forced young men who didn't want to teach into teaching, and into science, engineering, and other positions. Channelling involved deferments or alternatives to the draft for those who would take deferrable jobs. National service implies a permanent draft with some going into the military and others being forced to serve the national interest.

Our responsibility, if we still value freedom, is to end the military draft and to say "No" to all efforts to expand it into general conscription for labor purposes. Both Nazi Germany and Communist Russia have relied on compulsory labor camps. We do not want their equivalent here.

V

Pax Americana

(Christian Advocate, March 6, 1969)

More than two years ago, the Douglas Aircraft Corporation (now McDonnell-Douglas), at the request of the Army, completed a study which was originally entitled "Pax Americana." Later it was titled "— Strategic Alignments and Military Objectives." But its purpose was, in the Army's words, to find "a basis for the U.S. to maintain world hegemony in the future."

That study has never been declassified, in spite of a request by the chairman of the Senate Foreign Relations Committee, J. W. Fulbright. In refusing to declassify the study, Paul C. Warnke, assistant secretary of defense, wrote that "if the hypotheses, suggestions or conclusions contained in the study were construed as future policy of the U.S., the study would be susceptible to misinterpretations and could produce serious repercussions abroad."

The phrase "maintain world hegemony" is appropriate, since the United States is today the dominant economic and military factor throughout the non-Communist world. That dominance is reflected in the fact that American business plays a decisive role in many foreign countries. Total overseas U.S. business investments as of 1966 were $64.8 billion, more than the gross national product of most nations. In Britain, for example, U.S. firms own half of all modern industry.[1] Members of the Foreign Affairs Committee of Britain's House of Commons told me in 1966 that American control had reached the point where no British government could adopt a foreign policy independent of the United States.

In Canada the bulk of major manufacturing and mining is controlled by U.S. business.[2] Latin American investments by American business

---

[1] *Time,* December 29, 1967, p. 56.

[2] Edwin L. Dale, Jr., "The U.S. Economic Giant Keeps Growing," *New York Times Magazine,* March 19, 1967, p. 136.

totalled $10 billion as of 1967 with the yearly increase continuing at a rate of $400 million.[3]

One way in which control by the U.S. government is exercised in such countries is illustrated by action the Johnson administration took with respect to Belgian trade with Cuba. It forbade a Belgian company with 65 percent American ownership from selling $1.2 million worth of farm equipment to Cuba. The Cuban assets-control regulations of the U.S. require Treasury Department licenses for any exports to Cuba. Such regulations apply to companies in other countries where Americans hold more than 50 percent of the share of a foreign company. If the company nevertheless were to sell to Cuba without such a license, the American directors would be subject to prosecution for felonious action.

When questions were raised in the Belgian Parliament about why the company was being forced to lose the equivalent of 40 days' work for each of 2,400 workers because of American regulations, the Belgian government responded, "It is necessary to strike a balance between the loss of employment involved in this and the fact that workers in our country have benefited from foreign capital. We must not forget that."

A spokesman for the Sperry Rand Corporation, which was the company involved, said on February 6, 1968, "It is corporate policy to conduct all of its international affairs in full conformity with the policies of the United States Government.[4]

This kind of control, plus the more subtle control of an entire economy by outside firms who do not have a loyalty to the national interest of each country where they operate, has disturbed many statesmen in other nations. Britain's Prime Minister, Harold Wilson, for example, stated in an address to the Council of Europe in Strasbourg, while referring to membership in NATO, "Loyalty must never mean subservience. Still less must it mean an industrial helotry under which we in Europe produce only the conventional apparatus of a modern economy, while becoming increasingly dependent on American business for the sophisticated apparatus which will call the industrial tune in the seventies and eighties."[5]

President Charles de Gaulle of France at his semiannual news conference in 1967 referred to "an American takeover of our businesses . . ."

A little-known fact about American business expansion in Europe and Asia is the assistance given by the military. The Marshall Plan which strengthened the economy of Western Europe was the necessary forerunner of NATO. Although there were a number of reasons for domestic support of the Marshall Plan such as altruism in the churches and

---

[3] *New York Times*, January 22, 1968, p. 56.

[4] *New York Times*, February 7, 1968.

[5] Dale, op cit., p. 138.

self-interest by tobacco and cotton congressmen, to name only a few, one of the major reasons for this as a foreign policy was described at the time by a Scripps-Howard columnist, Cecil Dickson. He wrote of the fear held "by our foreign policy makers that the Western Europeans would seek to declare themselves neutral in event of war between the world's two giants." He described the "clamor in Britain, France and the Lowlands for a neutral status similar to that enjoyed by Eire during the late war and against granting the United States bases should conflict occur." Finally, he indicated that "by helping those countries to build up their economy, health, trade and business and improve their living conditions, our policy makers believe a fighting spirit can be regained."

The economic recovery stimulated by the Marshall Plan developed into a boom as American troops stationed in Europe under NATO provided American dollars for expansion.

American capital moved into Europe so rapidly after 1950 that by the summer of 1965 direct investments there reached a total of more than $12 billion, according to *Fortune*, "a 360 percent increase in only ten years time." In the five year period 1960-1965 American investment in West Germany went up about 165% to $2 billion. In France it increased 130% to $1.5 billion; in Italy 150% to $800 million; in the Netherlands 115% to $525 million; in Belgium and Luxembourg it almost doubled in going up to $430 million.[6]

U.S. direct investment in United Kingdom commerce and industry was estimated at $5.2 billion in 1965, up $600 million from 1964.[7]

There are still 340,000 American military personnel and 250,000 dependents plus thousands of American civilian employees of the armed forces in Western Europe. Senator Stephen Young in his July, 1968, newsletter refers to this as "foreign aid in disguise."

In Asia the same process has been at work. In the small country of Taiwan American investments reached $130 million by the end of 1967, chiefly in electronics, chemicals, and petrochemicals.[8] About 500 American manufacturers are doing business in Taiwan where the U.S. still maintains about 50,000 troops.

In Korea, where the U.S. maintains a troop strength of 50,000, the country is rapidly being tied to the American economy. Prior to 1966, 25 American companies with investments of $41 million were doing business. In 1966 representatives of more than 100 American companies visited Seoul to look into investment possibilities. Cotton textile manufacturing is the largest of all Korean industries. The Korean Cotton Textiles Export Association indicates that "we are required to buy

---

[6] *Fortune*, August, 1965 p. 126.

[7] James Reston, *Kansas City Times*, December 2, 1966.

[8] *New York Times*, January 19, 1968.

raw cotton . . . only from the U.S.A." This means that "all of the imported cotton comes from the United States. In 1967 Korea was able to import 387,814 bales of American cotton, costing $41,310,000 . . . and 49,000 bales of usual marketing requirement raw cotton, costing $6,370,000 from the U.S.A."[9]

The first American soldiers in Thailand arrived in 1950, but as of 1960 totalled only about 500 men. Since then the American military presence gradually expanded until it numbered 47,000 in May, 1968. The U.S. has invested almost a billion dollars in Thailand in five major U.S. Air Force bases with a sixth about half-built, a new seaport and an elaborate communications network linking Bangkok, Saigon, Manila, and the United States together. In addition there is an extensive new highway system built by U.S. taxes. As a result of this influx of aid, the U.S. has moved into second place in trade, with Japan still in first place. There has been an increase from a handful of U.S. firms doing business in Thailand in the postwar period to about 100 American corporations and affilliates in 1967.[10] Investment incentives include a profit return of 25 percent and more per year and low labor costs.[11]

The U.S. government has used another device for building American economic control. The U.S. Agency for International Development guarantees American investors up to 100 percent against losses through war, expropriation, insurrection, and currency incontrovertibility, and up to 75 percent against normal business risks. Such insurance has aided American business in Thailand, South Viet Nam, and elsewhere. Both the *Christian Science Monitor* and *Newsweek* reported in 1966 20 to 30 percent annual returns on investments in South Viet Nam.

On a world scale during the period 1950-65 about $13 billion more was returned to business firms in the U.S. from their overseas investments than they invested abroad from their own captial.[12]

The total earned income from all U.S. direct investments overseas in all industries was $6.4 billion in 1965. The value of direct investment abroad was 60.8% of the total U.S. private foreign investment in 1965.

According to the National Industrial Conference Board, "Repatriated dividends and interest, together with royalties and management fees, amounted to 76.1% of the income earned in all industries in 1965." This means that about $4 billion returned to the U.S. in 1965.

This exploitation of the economies of other countries is not new and the name "imperialism" given to it by others is not new. The dimensions, however, are so great as to signify the greatest economic control

9 Idem.
10 *Christian Science Monitor*, October 12, 1967.
11 *New York Times*, May 6, 1968.
12 Joseph D. Phillips, "The Dollar Invade Europe," *The Nation*, September 18, 1967.

of other nations by one nation in world history. McGeorge Bundy, until recently a key figure in the Johnson administration, revealed that the military industrial alliance is worldwide. He said: "More than four-fifths of all the foreign investing in the world is now done by Americans . . . We no longer doubt that we should have extensive actions in Europe, in South America, in Asia, and in all oceans . . . We must put troops where they are most needed."

The Pax Americana pattern that has developed is one of U.S. business and military cooperation to provide a more stable world control than colonialism as such would permit. Indigenous businessmen in each country are invited to take top posts with American firms so that they develop a vested interest in American business activity in their country. The same is true also of many workers. Standard Oil of New Jersey, for example, employs in its overseas executive group 121 Americans, four Canadians, one Venezuelan, 86 Britons, 21 Germans, 16 Frenchmen, 14 Italians, 10 Belgians, 10 Norwegians, 10 Swedes, eight Dutchmen, two Danes, two Swiss, one Finn, and one Maltese.[13]

The combination of American military garrisons around the world, "legalized" by the various military alliances in which the U.S. is the major factor, and the American owned businesses that have been merged with the local and national power structures, is the key to American world control. But there are more than military and business interests involved. The Institute for International Education helps tie educational institutions and scholars to the American overseas program. The Institute provides a service to corporations such as Esso, Chrysler, General Electric, Proctor and Gamble, Ford, and Xerox. This includes the providing of a roster of foreign students and scholars studying, teaching, or doing research in the U.S., a similar roster of U.S. scholars abroad, and screening and placement of foreign students in colleges with scholarship provided by tax-deductible contributions from the corporations.

The reason for bringing foreign students to the U.S., according to an article in I.B.M.'s *Think* is that "foreign students will ultimately be helpful to U.S. business." Referring to the merging of the American and local power structures, *Think* adds that "American corporations, gradually turning their operations in foreign countries over to the people who live there, will need trained personnel." The Institute, in explaining its usefulness to the American investing program, asserts in a promotional pamphlet: "In the last decade U.S. corporations have expanded their direct foreign investments by 60 percent—to $40 billion at the end of 1963. They recognize abroad as well as at home—that education offers the best means for stimulating purchasing power, encouraging political

---

[13] *Time,* December 29, 1967, p. 58.

stability, and most important of all, developing a reservoir of the trained manpower so necessary to their overseas operations."

The cold war has for many years provided the political and military rationale for foreign aid, for maintaining troops overseas, and for building huge military bases abroad. It also is the basis for the huge taxation of civilians which is transferred to the military and in turn to large corporations doing business with the military. John Galbraith, the Harvard economist and former U.S. Ambassador, wrote that "the relation of the Cold War to the needs of the industrial system is remarkably close." Although the competition between the U.S. and the U.S.S.R. was not entirely one-sided, Galbraith added that "the weapons competition, and the image of international relations on which it depended, originated partly in the industrial system . . ."

It is possible to assert that the Pax Americana is simply a response to the world Communist threat, but it is also possible to indicate that the cold war was a convenient necessity to enable the military-industrial complex to expand around the world with support of the American taxpayer.

VI

The Political Power of Multinational Corporations

(The Christian Century, September 25, 1974)

U.S. Foreign policy is increasingly being shaped by multinational corporations. There are more than 4,000 U.S. companies that can be classified as multinational, and the largest of them have worldwide sales of from $3 billion to $30 billion a year.

One way in which these multinationals influence foreign policy is through their overseas operations. International Telephone and Telegraph, for example, is the world's fifth-largest employer, with operations in 67 nations on five continents; and some of its employees, says Willard F. Mueller, former chief economist of the Federal Trade Commission,

> are better known in circles of international diplomacy than in business. They have included such notables as former UN Secretary-General Trygve Lie as a director of ITT Norway and one-time Belgium Premier Paul-Henri Spaak as a director of ITT Belgium. It is not unfair to ask, are such men on ITT's board because of their business acumen or their prestige in international diplomacy? This raises a corollary question of who is more powerful in international diplomacy, the U.S. State Department or huge international conglomerates like ITT?

Norway and Belgium are by no means the only countries in which influential political figures are ITT directors. In France, Armand-Gaston de Bonneval, formerly an aide to President Charles de Gaulle, is on the board of the ITT subsidiary, Materiel Telephonique; and in Britain, Lord Caccia, a former ambassador to the United States, is chairman of the ITT subsidiary in his nation. Standard Oil of New Jersey (Exxon) employs in its overseas executive group 121 Americans, four Canadians, one Venezuelan, 86 Britons, 21 Germans, 16 Frenchmen, 14 Italians, 10 Belgians, 10 Norwegians, 10 Swedes, eight Dutchmen, two Danes, two Swiss, one Finn and one Maltese. Europe's leading elder statesman, Paul Henri Spaak, is also connected with Standard Oil.

In 1969, while teaching in Buenos Aires, I came across *Contra la Ocupacion Extranjera*, a book published a year earlier. It described the relationship of leading members of the Argentine ruling elite to corporations doing business in their country. At that time Argentina was governed by a coalition of generals and admirals, and the book concluded with a six-page list of high-ranking retired military officers who were head or directors of such corporations.

Working through the important indigenous business, politcal and military figures their foreign subsidiaries employ, the multinational corporations exercise tremendous influence on government policy in the various nations. What this setup represents is a merger of the power-elites of the American business world with the power-elites of other countries, so that their financial interests become identical. Hence they are often able to prevent adverse governmental moves, such as expropriation.

Many of the multinational corporations have excellent communications and intelligence networks. ITT's network is probably the most effective. Every month American ITT executives fly in a chartered Pan American plane to Brussels where they meet with ITT executives from Europe, Africa and the Middle East to review the operations of each company and assess political and economic trends. Is there any threat of nationalizations? Is anti-American sentiment rising or subsiding? Will the dollar go down in value, and, if so, how can dollar losses be avoided? The monthly area staff meetings held in various regions — e.g., Africa or the Middle East — supply some of the data considered at Brussels. Thanks to its thorough study of all political and economic factors affecting its operations, ITT is at least as well informed as most governments about what is going on in the world.

I

Take recent events in Chile, where ITT has — or had — a $200 million investment. The corporation was well aware that if Allende became Chile's president its investment would be threatened. Therefore, early in 1970, it tried to persuade the CIA and the Nixon administration to take steps to prevent the election of Allende. The attempt failed, and Allende was voted into office in November. A few months later — in mid-1971 — ITT adopted a new tactic and began urging the Nixon administration to work for the overthrow of the Allende government. In September, 1971, Harold Geneen, ITT president and chief executive officer, met over lunch with Peter Peterson, Mr. Nixon's assistant for international affairs, to discuss the Chilean situation. On September 29, ITT in Chile was expropriated. On October 1, William Merriam, an

ITT vice-president, wrote Peterson ("Dear Pete") outlining the course of action the corporation wanted the U.S. to follow. Merriam proposed that the administration halt the flow to Chile of U.S. aid funds (about $1 million a month) and stop the U.S. contributions through the Inter-American Development Bank for earthquake relief in Chile. He suggested that "as many U.S. markets as possible should be closed in Chile" and that "any U.S. exports of special importance to Allende should be delayed or stopped."

In short, the ITT strategy was to promote economic unrest in Chile by cutting off all loans and credit and at the same time refusing to buy from or sell key products to Chile. Later that month (October, 1971) an assistant secretary of the treasury, referring to the cutting off of aid to Chile, said, "The Nixon administration is a business administration. Its mission is to protect business." On January 19, 1972, President Nixon himself announced the policy decision with respect to Chile:

> . . . when a country expropriates a significant U.S. interest without making reasonable provision for such compensation to U.S. citizens, we will presume that the U.S. will not extend new bilateral economic benefits to the expropriating country . . . and . . . in the face of the expropriatory circumstances just described we will presume that the U.S. government will withhold its support from loans . . . in multilateral development banks.

Subsequently, ITT reported to the White House that "there is a beginning of concern on the part of the military" in Chile and that the military "realize that, before economic chaos takes place, the armed forces will have to step in and restore order."

The administration accepted the ITT strategy of encouraging a military takeover of the Chilean government by promoting economic unrest. It cut off all loans and credit. Chile couldn't even get credit to buy replacement parts for its U.S. built buses, and over 2,000 buses in the capital city of Santiago were out of commission. Other multinational corporations also fell in with the ITT strategy, and the World Bank, which is largely under U.S. control, refused aid. Meanwhile, the Nixon administration increased military aid to the Chilean armed forces from $800,000 the year before the expropriation to $5.7 million in 1971, $12.3 million in 1973.

II

Various groups in Chile, including the churches, realized that these moves, taken at the behest of ITT, might well lead to civil war. In the Spring of 1973, Raimundo Valenzuela, a former Methodist bishop in Chile, appeared at the ITT annual stockholders meeting in Kansas City to speak of the "outrage all Chileans feel at the damage ITT was willing to inflict upon our nation." Harold Geneen defended the ITT policy by saying, "I am sorry we were not able to persuade the government to take a stronger stand in Chile." The audience of 500 stockholders applauded enthusiastically, and then re-elected to the ITT board John A. McCone, the former CIA director who had offered the U.S. government $1 million to block Allende's election.

Among the multinational corporations falling in with the ITT strategy were the Kennecott Corporation and Anaconda Copper. In February, 1972, they moved to attach Chile's assets in the United States. In September, 1972 Kennecott asked a French court to block payment for Chilean copper sold in France, and took similar action in Sweden, Italy and Germany. This tactic not only forced Chile to spend more than $150,000 in legal fees overseas, but it also intimidated potential creditors, with the result that Chile was unable to complete negotiations for credit from European banks. Some corporations cooperated with ITT by charging Chile higher prices and demanding cash payments in European currencies in advance. Five major New York banks also stopped credits for Chile.

As foreseen, the economic and political action of the multinational corporations and the U.S. government created chaos in Chile. On September 11, 1973, the military seized the reins.

III

The multinational corporations, however, have subtler ways of influencing American foreign policy—for instance, through their participation in the financing and operations of the Council on Foreign Relations. The council, a research and discussion group founded in 1921 to provide information about foreign affairs, brings together corporation executives, government officials, military officers and scholars in study groups of about 25 persons each, which consider specific problems in the field of foreign affairs and suggest strategies for dealing with them. It was the Council on Foreign Relations that laid the groundwork for the United Nations Charter, the Marshall Plan, NATO, the cold war and, more recently, the changed U.S. policy with respect to China. And it was from the council that, during World War II, industry drew the executives it needed. As John J. McCloy, former chairman of Chase Manhattan Bank, a trustee of the Ford Foundation, and director of the Council on Foreign Relations, said, "Whenever we needed a man we thumbed through the roll of council members and put through a call to New York." In 1942, personnel from the council were taken into the State Department as the nucleus of the Advisory Committee on Post-War Planning.

In this connection mention must be made of the Committee for Economic Development organized by former secretary of Commerce Jesse Jones, Paul Hoffman of Studebaker Corporation, and William Benton of the Encyclopaedia Britannica, and made up of bankers, economists and corporation executives. It was from this and similar groups that Paul Hoffman drew the men to administer the Marshall Plan when he became its chief administrator.

The key policy-making positions in the U.S. government are held by people from the Council on Foreign Relations, the Committee for Economic Development, and the various corporations related to these. Between 1940 and 1968, almost every U.S. secretary and deputy secretary of defense, almost every secretary of Army, Navy and Air Force, and almost every CIA director and chairman of the Atomic Energy Commission was recruited from the corporations and the financial institutions involved with them. It is this interlocking directorate of government and business which makes it easy for the multinational corporations to lobby their former colleagues, who already share their point of view.

That means that basic foreign policy is not determined by Congress or even by the State Department. In the United States, political and economic power are fused. The fundamental decisions are made by the managers of the multinational corporations in combination with their counterparts in the political and military bureaucracy.

The multinationals are not always in agreement among themselves or with the bureaucrats, but there is general agreement that business must be involved in foreign policy and that government has an essential role in maintaining the world capitalist system and U.S. business dominance in that system. As former Secretary of State Dean Rusk put it in a statement to Senate Committee on Foreign Relations in 1968, ". . . our influence is used wherever it can be and persistently through embassies on a day-to-day basis, in our aid discussions, and in direct negotiations to underline the importance of private investment." The multinational corporation is the single most powerful unit within the private investment system, and, collectively, giant multinationals exert pressures upon and provide personnel for government in the conduct of foreign policy. Thus the national interest becomes a euphemism for the collective interest of the multinational corporations.

VII

The War System Is The Enemy

(*Fellowship*, October, 1977)

Neither the United States nor the Soviet Union wants disarmament. This is unfortunately true not only of those in government, but also of the people of both countries, where the overwhelming majority still believe that national security rests on military preparedness. yet the same people are uneasy about the danger of nuclear war, so that their leaders must continue to give assurances that they are working toward disarmament and that each new weapons system that goes into production is only to deter the enemy from attacking.

From the time the bomb was developed, every U.S. President, beginning with Harry Truman, has urged some form of nuclear disarmament, but never with any real intent to disarm. In fact, both in 1955 and in 1958, when, after much negotiation, the Soviet Union had apparently accepted U.S. proposals for general and complete disarmament, the U.S. withdrew the proposals. The whole idea of disarmament had been a public relations device, designed to fool the American people. Since then, all proposals and negotiations have been for arms control, which includes such devices as a partial ban on nuclear weapons tests and the limitation of the numbers of certain types of weapons.

President Carter, who operates in this tradition, has no intention of seeking general and complete disarmament. Not only has he made no such proposal, but he has asked for authority to build the neutron bomb. He has decided to go ahead on the Cruise Missile, as well. Moreover, the clearest picture of where Mr. Carter stands can be seen in his failure to counter the growing anti-Soviet hysteria generated by the extreme right and by the military-industrial establishment. This hysteria is designed to put pressure on the Congress and the President to increase America's nuclear arms arsenal.

To counterbalance this pressure, some anti-war organizations poured an enormous amount of time and resources into opposing the B-1. But the president's decision to shelve the B-1 was not made in response to the sustained campaign against it; it was a military judgment conveyed to Carter by Secretary of Defense Harold Brown, that B-52's with Cruise Missiles would be a more effective and less costly way to penetrate Soviet air defenses. The significance of Carter's decision in favor of Cruise Missiles, with their ominous, first strike implications, is seen in a Soviet commentary that the "production of the Cruise Missile . . . means virtually the discovery of a new fourth channel of the strategic arms race" along with the intercontinental ballistic missiles, submarine launched missiles, and heavy bombers.

Carter's request that Congress let him decide on the production of the neutron weapon has been put in the propaganda context of implying that if the U.S. threatens to produce neutron warheads, the Soviet Union will recognize the need to come to terms with U.S. arms control proposals. But it has also been set in the context of deterrence. The neutron warhead is designed not to destroy property but to kill soldiers with lethal radiation that is short-lived, so that "friendly" troops could move into a battlefield area within hours or days, rather than months. This, says the Pentagon, will deter a Soviet attack on Germany. The significance of the neutron weapon is that it introduces nuclear weapons into conventional war planning. It is intended to make the use of nuclear weapons palatable to the American people by advertising them for use against enemy soldiers instead of civilian populations. The soldiers would die slowly and painfully from radiation. As for civilians, Senator Mark Hatfield (R., Ore.) presented evidence in the Senate debate that a concentrated series of neutron explosions would create a radioactive cloud of carbon that would immediately threaten civilian populations.

The further significance of both the cruise missile and the neutron weapon is that the Soviet Union will rush to produce these and other new weapons to counter the U.S. lead; thus we will face an accelerated arms race. Would the U.S. bow to distasteful Soviet arms control proposals if Russia had developed a new horror weapon or would the Pentagon rush to build its own new carriers of death? The Soviet military response is likely to be the same as that of the Pentagon. And Soviet spokesmen have said this would be the case.

Another action of the Carter administration belies his talks of arms reduction, specifically at the point of reducing arms sales abroad. He has increased the military assistance program to the Philippines in spite of official State Department reports about human rights abuses there. He has authorized arms for the neighbors of Ethiopia, which has moved out of the U.S. orbit into that of the Soviet Union. One of these neighbors, Somalia, already heavily armed by the Soviet Union, has launched a major military offensive against Ethiopia. Thus, the Administration is getting its revenge against Ethiopia for leaving the American sphere of influence and, at the same time, helping to fuel a proxy war against the Soviet Union through its new satellite, Ethiopia.

Carter also proposed a sale of sixty F-15 fighters to Saudi Arabia, while offering to sell a modern airborne radar warning system to Iran, Saudi Arabia's enemy.

One of the chief arguments used in Washington to justify selling weapons to the nations of the Third World is that if we don't, the Soviet Union or China will. An excellent counter argument was given by John Kenneth Galbraith to the Senate Foreign Relations Committee April 25, 1966.

> It was Soviet tanks that surrounded Ben Bella's palace in Algiers when that Soviet supported leader was thrown out. It was a Soviet and Chinese equipped army which deposed the Indonesian Communists, destroyed the Communist Party and which left Sukarno's vision of an Asian socialism in shambles. It was a Soviet trained pretorian guard which was expected to supply the ultimate protection to the government of President Nkrumah, and which did not. One can only conclude that those who worry about Soviet arms wish to keep the Russians out of trouble.

In some respects the most serious indication of the Carter Administration's long range position is the silence in the face of demands for rearmament based on allegations that the Soviet Union is becoming Number One. Three groups are chiefly responsible for this pressure: the Pentagon; the right wing American Security Council with headquarters in Boston, Virginia, and a membership of industrialists and retired top military personnel; and the Committee of the Present Danger, composed of America's defense intellectuals, many of whom held government positions during the Cold War. These groups have a common line: that the Soviet Union is either gaining on the U.S. or surpassing it in armaments, and that the U.S. must substantially expand its military budget to stay ahead.

Their campaign was begun to forestall any cutbacks in troops and arms following the Vietnam War. The Gallup Poll revealed the mood of the American people prior to their campaign, when nearly half (44 percent) of all persons interviewed in 1974 said they believed that U.S. was spending too much on the military.

James Schlesinger, now a member of Carter's cabinet and formerly President Ford's Secretary of Defense, launched the campaign for a larger military budget. He wrote the Senate Appropriations Committee in October, 1975, that "by most available measures American power is declining and Soviet power is rising." The best estimate is that military spending exceeds that of the U.S. by "as much as 50 percent" if retirement pay is excluded, he said.

Schlesinger, the CIA, and other top military figures joined in misleading Congress and the people by using a spurious device. They estimated what it would cost in dollars at current U.S. prices to pay for the Soviet armed forces. They computed the pay scale of Soviet soldiers at the rate of pay of American troops. Wrote Rep. Les Aspin (D., Wis.): "The absurdity of this calculation is obvious: if Congress voted to cut U.S. salaries back to the pre-volunteer Army pay rates, the Soviet military 'budget' would plummet overnight."

Nevertheless, Congress went right along with the Schlesinger-CIA advice and expanded the military budget. One factor in the expansion was the Navy propaganda for more ships. Between 1970 and 1975, the Navy loaned, sold, or gave away 272 ships to other countries. The transfer process was still going on in 1976, when the Pentagon was deploring the fact that the U.S. Navy had been cut from 800 ships to 479 and insisting that the Soviet naval threat called for a U.S. fleet of at least 600 ships. The Pentagon told Congress in 1976 that the Soviet Union had outbuilt the U.S. between 1965 and 1975, with 205 "major surface combatants" compared to 165 built by the U.S., giving the Soviets a 20 percent edge.

Asked to supply a breakdown of ships above or below 3,000 tons, the Chief of Naval Operations pleaded that the information was classified. One Senator, Patrick Leahy of Vermont, by sheer persistence discovered the truth — that in 15 years, the U.S. had built 122 "major surface combatants" of 3,000 tons or more, while the Soviet Union had built 57. The Navy had been comparing small Soviet escort vessels of less than 3,000 tons with large U.S. ships.

Unfortunately, the Carter Administration has done nothing to expose this kind of misleading propaganda. Effective exposés appeared in the April 3, 1976, *Nation*, in the April, 1977, *Bulletin of the Atomic Scientists*, and in publications of the Center for Defense Information. The United Church of Christ also published an effective analysis: "Are the Russians Really Coming?"

Where do we stand? It seems clear that there will be no disarmament by the military-industrial complex or the President as Commander-in-Chief of the complex. Nor will there be serious negotiations with other nations unless the people demand disarmament. The Administration will try to make it appear that something is being accomplished at the arms control talks. In reality, arms control talks serve as a cover for the strengthening of military machines; they allow for discussion, but never action, on the mutual reduction of arms. Gerard C. Smith, who was chief of the U.S. delegation at the Strategic Arms Limitation Talks

(SALT) from 1969 to 1972, admitted as much. "In effect we were trying to get an arrangement that would limit Soviet modernization programs, but not our own," he said. "We are trying to fix constraints on Soviet programs that would not affect American programs."

As recently as last August, the U.S. representative at the 30-nation Geneva Disarmament Conference rejected Soviet proposals for a comprehensive international treaty banning new weapons of mass destruction. The U.S. position is that the best approach is separate agreements outlawing specific weapons, once they become public knowledge. But in practice the U.S. is not prepared to ban new weapons on which it has a monopoly or any qualitative superiority.

The only way the American people can get their government to negotiate seriously for disarmament is to be willing to seek unilateral disarmament. They must be unmoved by Pentagon propaganda about Russian superiority, or who is Number One. They must not concentrate on banning the production of one weapon, whether B-1 or Cruise Missile or Neutron Bomb; the Pentagon can always come up with something new to fuel the war system.

We must recognize that in the nuclear age the war system is the enemy. People everywhere have everything to lose and nothing to gain by its continuance. If a nation were completely disarmed and therefore no threat to any nuclear power, there would be no reason for any nation to want to destroy it. But if nuclear war came and that nation were armed, it would be destroyed, regardless of the size or effectiveness of its armed forces.

Americans view the Russians as enemies, not because they are Communists, but because they have the armed capability of conquering and destroying other nations. We would not fear a completely disarmed Soviet Union; they would not fear a disarmed United States.

Our goal is world disarmament, but unless hundreds of thousands of the people in each nation work to disarm their own country, governments will never negotiate seriously for universal disarmament. So long as people are prepared to accept armed forces, we cannot expect their governments to disarm. When, and only when, the people are prepared to disarm unilaterally, governments will be unable to use other nations as convenient excuses for their own unwillingness to disarm.

VIII

Is It Police Action

(*Zion's Herald*, December 26, 1951)

"When he was accused, as he was over and over again by his enemies, that he was a friend of sinners, that he consorted with these people who were outcasts of society, he said, 'Why, these people are sick and when a doctor comes, he goes to the sick people; he doesn't go to the well people!"

"This is The Day,"
Theodore P. Ferris,
Wilcox and Follette Co., New York

Recently both Russia and the United States have begun to use the word "police" to apply to armies. The German army in the Soviet zone is being given military training and has military weapons, but is called a police force. A group of 75,000 Japanese, armed and given military training by the American occupation army, is called a police force. The war in Korea was termed police action against North Korean invaders who wouldn't obey a United Nations order. Finally, on September 19, 1950, Secretary of State Dean Acheson asked the United Nations for a police force to be formed from the armies of member states.

Is this a confusion of words or is police action somehow synonymous with army action? Or is it possible that the use of the word "police" lends a legal character to what would otherwise be a typical military venture? If we think for a few minutes of the respect usually accorded the police and the function which the police perform in society, we can more easily note the distinction between the police and the army. A police force is an asset to the average city and state. In addition to directing traffic, escorting distinguished visitors, aiding at accidents and fires, the police are expected to enforce the law against the few who choose to violate the will of the community. The police are, generally speaking, so essential to the orderly running of a complex society that the mere mention of "police action" connotes law and order.

Although soldiers are present in increasing numbers in modern society, they are not essential to anything except the waging of war. Despite the fact that both the soldier and the policeman wear uniforms, they have characteristic functions which distinguish them from each other and which make army action and police action completely different in purpose, operation, and effect. A police force, for instance, operates against wrongdoers but not against their innocent families and friends. An army, on the other hand, acts against a whole nation, irrespective of the guilt or innocence of its inhabitants. A police force is responsible to the community whose laws it enforces, whereas an army tries to enforce its will on other communities. The police of New York, for example, deal with criminals in New York; they do not fight the police of Philadelphia.

The authority of the police is limited to making an arrest and they may use only as much force as is required to make the arrest. Thereafter the person arrested is entitled to trial by jury and if guilty is sentenced by an impartial judge. An army, however, uses indiscriminate force to inflict its will, acting as judge, jury and executioner of masses of people.

A police force can operate effectively only with the consent of the community. Eighteen thousand policemen in New York City can enforce laws only if the great majority of eight million New Yorkers approve those laws and obey them. Police action is therefore necessarily limited in its application to individuals and small groups who violate law. When very large groups in a community or state are aroused to the point of organized resistance to law, a wise government will try to correct the injustice that caused the resentment rather than attempt by armed action to enforce its will. An army is not needed and has no reason for existence in a society where consent really operates. An army's chief function is to impose its will on those people who will not give their ready consent to the decisions of those who are in command and control of the army that wishes to rule over them.

The use of soldiers rather than police is therefore evidence of the weakness of the society that uses them. A government with real power does not need to put on a show of force, but a state that is weak must constantly display what power it has. It is obvious, for example, that an unarmed London "bobby" expresses more real power than the well-armed Italian police. The London police base their power on the consent and cohesion of the English people, whereas the Italian government is much weaker in terms of such consent.

Governments can achieve real power and strength not by using soldiers or even by arming and expanding the police force but by action which meets the political, economic and spiritual needs of the people. That action will build cohesion and support of government and, as in England today, make revolt of the people a political impossibility. Similarly, on a world scale, cohesion and support of people throughout the world can be built in proportion to the U.N.'s policies and actions which really meet the needs of the masses of people in China, India, Africa, Russia, and South America, as well as in Western Europe.

No organized community can have law and order and at the same time permit two centers of power to exist within it. For example, no community could have two opposing police forces. A police force, to be effective, must work in what is essentially an unarmed community. If the citizens of the community are armed, they must be armed only as individuals — viz., game hunters, and not as gangs or organized units.

Armies justify their existence because there are other armies. On a world level police action would be possible only if there were no rival centers of power, or, in other words, if there were no armies. A disarmed world is thus the prerequisite for a world police force or international police action on a world scale. Army action and police action differ also in terms of results. Although the police may occasionally incur the life-long resentment of a person they have arrested or injured, the result of police action in a community or state tends to strengthen the process of, and increase respect for, law and order. Army action generally arouses such widespread resentment and hostility as to nullify most of the gains the army sought to accomplish. One has only to remember that the "solid South" is a creature of the resentment in the South at the Northern armies and the policies they enforced. In the world in which we live no useful purpose is served by calling a soldier a policeman. Police action is quite different from army action or war, and its identification with war will only make it more difficult to achieve the kind of world society where there will be policemen instead of soldiers.

Even if we recognize that the action in Korea was war and that Mr. Acheson's proposal for a U.N. police force is really a proposal for a U.N. army, we still have the question: Will not such army action strengthen the U.N. and help achieve world government? Army action in the first instance presupposes an enemy army that must be defeated. At the present time the U.N. is divided, with nations representing about half the world's population generally voting on "security" matters against a smaller group of nations who claim the allegiance of about 40 percent of the world's population. If army action were fully used by both sides, there would be a world war and an end to the U.N., even if the army of one side were called a U.N. force. In practice, the world would be divided against itself, and all that would be left would be military alliances on each side, even if called by a sweeter name.

Even in the event that a U.N. army is used only in localized wars, viz., Korea, nationalism is more likely to be strengthened than is the U.N. Both in Korea and in the Acheson plan for a U.N. army, the basis of the U.N. armed force is a group of national units or armies. Partly this is because of the present strength of nationalism. Men fight better for traditional loyalties and for a cause that is identified with home. But the continuance of national armies and national loyalties also tends to strengthen nationalism at the expense of a world loyalty. Furthermore, the development of a U.N. army, as Mr. Acheson proposes, would give moral support to American militarism, since the United States, as the "biggest" power in the "loyal" U.N. bloc, would be expected to provide the military leadership, most of the weapons, and the bulk of the manpower for such an army. Already in anticipation of this the Pentagon has asked for and has been granted 3,500,000 men who will perform traditional American military functions as well as U.N. army functions when "invited" to do so.

A more fundamental reason for national units is that no nation is or ever will be willing to turn over soldiers to a world force that will function as an army against its own national government. For this further reason, no U.N. army can fulfill a police function of impartially operating against nations which violate law. If a nation like the United States were willing to submit to U.N. law, there would be no need of a U.N. army to deal with the United States. A police force would be sufficient to deal with individual Americans who violated U.N. laws. If the U.S. would not submit to U.N. law and a U.N. army tried to enforce its will, there would be a war. Substitute the word "Russia" for "United States" and the results would be the same.

Properly speaking, the use of national units upon vote of a group of nations who would contribute them is a military alliance. This is true not only because they are national units but because they would be used arbitrarily as their national governments together decided. They would not, for example, act automatically and impartially to enforce law on their own nations.

Not only would a U.N. army cause division and eventual war among the nations in the United Nations, but it would set back the cause of world government by acting on the false assumption that states can be coerced into cooperation by war. James Madison made this point in the Constitutional Convention when it was proposed that states in the Federal Union be coerced into obeying Federal law. "He observed that the more he reflected upon the use of force, the more he doubted the practicability, the justice and the efficacy of it when applied to people collectively, and not individually . . . A Union of the States (containing such an ingredient) seemed to provide for its own destruction. The use of force against a State, would look more like a declaration of war, than an infliction of punishment, and would probably be considered by the party attacked as a dissolution of all previous compacts by which it might be bound."

Alexander Hamilton similarly indicated that a government which enforced its laws by going to war was an irresponsible government. He asked, "Can any reasonable man be well disposed towards a government which makes war and carnage the only means of supporting itself – a government that can exist only by the sword? Every such war must involve the innocent with the guilty. The single consideration should be sufficient to dispose every peaceable citizen against such a government."

The principle of non-coercion of states has been generally accepted in the United States from that day to this. One major exception was the Civil War, which though fought to preserve unity of government, did more than anything else to keep the nation politically, economically, and racially divided in the decades that followed. That Civil War might never have occurred if the United States, after having established the principle of non-coercion of states, had made it impossible for member states to have their own militia. Because states did have their own militia, any group of them could set up another center of power to challenge the authority of the Federal government and could almost at a moment's notice direct their armies against those of other states.

John Dewey has summed up probably better than anyone else the mood of America as a result of our Civil War experience: "I think no reasonable person will hold that the coercive force of the Federal government is chiefly or in any large degree that which keeps the various states together; or that it is a factor of any great importance as compared with the bonds of common tradition, habit of mind, beliefs, information, inter-communication, commerce, etc., which tie the people of the states together. Nor can I imagine any sensible person today who, when he looks at rivalries of interest and latent friction between sections which still exist, would urge as a remedy the strenghening of coercive force exercised from above upon them (We tried 'force bills' after the Civil War). I cannot imagine such a person proposing anything but means which will positively intensify the bonds of common interest and purpose which exist among sections . . . Laws that are enforced are enforced because there is a community consensus behind them. The threat of force does not bring about consensus."

The U.N. can be strengthened only if it can achieve total world disarmament. So long as its member nations have armies to use against each other, it will be a house divided against itself. If the U.N. has an army of its own and any other armies exist to challenge its authority, there will be war. If no armies exist to challenge its authority, the U.N. will need no army and can proceed to enforce international law by police action directed toward individuals.

IX

The Case for Disarmament

(The Progressive, April, 1960)

Soviet Premier Nikita Khruschchev's address to the United Nations last September made disarmament a subject of renewed discussion and hope. It was at a moment of statlemate in the international scene, and after a long record of failure to achieve even a measure of disarmament, the Soviet Premier made his dramatic proposal for the world-wide elimination of armaments.

The proposal was hailed immediately by those who saw in it the hope of ending war and shifting the struggle between East and West to a nonmilitary competition. Some saw it as an indication the Russians were ready to renounce direct military control over Eastern Europe if the West were prepared to abandon its military control over colonies and over its bases scattered throughout the world. In the underdeveloped world it was viewed as the one realistic way to release the billions of dollars and rubles and pounds and francs needed for construction and economic development.

Only a day before the Khrushchev address, Selwyn Lloyd, the British Foreign Secretary, made an important similar proposal to the United Nations, calling for disarmament "down to internal policing levels." But it did not receive the attention the world gave to the Soviet proposal, chiefly because Britain is not the acknowledged military leader of either the Eastern or Western bloc.

In the United States the Khruschchev proposal aroused great interest precisely because the Soviet Union is our adversary in the cold war and our competitor in the arms race. The nation's press, however, was swift and outspoken in its criticism. In general, nine major criticisms have been leveled against the Khrushchev proposal and against disarmament in general.

One — Khruschchev didn't say anything new. He simply dusted off the old Soviet proposals made by Litvinov in 1927.

It is true, of course, that the two proposals are similar in that both of them called for total disarmament to be carried out in stages over a four-year period. But there are some important differences.

In 1927, the Soviet Union was weak and the Western nations were the great powers of the world. The Litvinov proposal was viewed then as a method for increasing the relative strength of the Soviet Union by eliminating the military might of the West. Today, the U.S.S.R. is a great power and is proposing the elimination of its own great military machine as well as those in the West.

Litvinov made his proposal when there was still fear of a German power revival that might result in war against France. This was an important factor in French opposition to disarmament, and France was one of the two most powerful nations in Europe. Today, France and Germany are working together. The danger from Germany is that she might precipitate a war between Russia and America. In fact the Russian fear of the rearmament of Germany is undoubtedly one of the reasons for the current Soviet proposal.

The Litvinov plan, if it had been accepted, would have spelled the end of British, French, Dutch, and other forms of colonialism maintained by armed force. None of the great powers, except the United States, was prepared then to yield empire because it would have weakened their great power status. Today, most colonies either are free or are in the process of achieving freedom. The mother country is not only aware of the inevitability of ultimate freedom but would profit more from not having to pay a heavy arms bill than it would from colonial investments. Disarmament would also enhance the relative power status of such second- and third-rate powers as Britain, France, Germany, Holland and Italy.

The greatest difference between 1927 and 1959 is that arms then could be used in war without destroying civilization and annihilating the nations engaged in such conventional hostilities. Today we live in the nuclear age. Disarmament is therefore simply a recognition that preparation for a war we dare not wage is too hazardous to continue.

Two — It is argued that the Russians will not accept inspection. While it is true they have dragged their feet on inspection proposals thus far, Khrushchev quite frankly pointed out in his speech that the Soviet Union had feared inspection coupled with only partial disarmament would provide merely "for the collection of intelligence information" which enemy states could then use. But if disarmament were complete "the states will have nothing to conceal from one another any more." Therefore "general and complete disarmament . . . will remove all the barriers that were raised during the consideration of questions of partial disarmament."

Khrushchev did not elaborate on the details of inspection during the first three stages. He simply spoke of a system of international control to "function in conformity with the stages by which disarmament should be effected." It is obvious, then, that only the most serious negotiations on our part will reveal whether the Russians are prepared to have adequate inspection at each stage. If they were convinced that we intended to press for complete disarmament and were in fact already planning for economic change to a peacetime economy, they would have evidence of our intentions sufficient to inspire confidence in adequate inspection at each stage.

Three—The Khrushchev proposal was criticized on the grounds that it is utopian to think of total disarmament, that it is only excessive arms that endanger us. Two questions are here involved. The first is whether the Soviet Union and other nations are ready to disarm. The second is whether disarmament by stages constitutes a realistic road to the ultimate goal.

The first question can be answered only tentatively since much depends on public opinion, the vested interests in military establishments, and a recognition by statesmen that nuclear war can never defend, but will only destroy, those who engage in it. The second question is answered by the fact that only when nations are convinced that satisfactory reduction of arms has taken place in stage one will they move on to the other stages. Thus the only fresh element in the current proposal is that, unlike previous plans, reduction of arms is seen not as an end in itself but as a step-by-step process toward complete disarmament.

Khrushchev therefore rightly criticized partial disarmament. "Apprehensions would always exist," he said, "that with the aid of the remaining types of armaments and armed forces the possibility of launching an attack would continue extant."

What is certainly utopian is to believe that there is a cause-and-effect relationship between the possession of weapons and the maintenance of peace. Such thinking overlooks the frequency with which wars have been started by blunder and miscalculation and assumes that arms will deter because calm, peace-loving, and rational statesmen will always be in control in each of the many nations of the world.

Four—A more important criticism of the Soviet proposal is the assertion that "you can't negotiate with the U.S.S.R. because she won't keep her agreements." Great power states, not the least of them the Soviet Union, have a record of breaking agreements that it is not in their interest to keep. After insisting in 1945 that Japan and Germany be disarmed and agree not to re-arm, the United States has insisted that they re-arm. Britain and France broke the United Nations Charter when they sent armies into the Suez area. The Soviet Union has likewise broken agreements. But the Soviets, just as other nations, keep agreements which are in their interest to keep. The Soviet Union has kept the agreement with the United States to withdraw troops from Austria and respect that country's neutrality. Similarly, the Finnish-Russian treaty continues to be observed. The problem in negotiating a disarmament agreement is to devise one that will be in the interests of both Russia and the West. Total disarmament and the chance to build and maintain economic and political systems free from the crushing burden of arms would be in the interests of all. Serious problems will be encountered in negotiating such an agreement, but none that is insuperable.

Five — It is said that the Soviet Union is not interested in disarmament or it would have accepted the Baruch Plan. The Baruch proposal in June, 1946, provided for an International Atomic Development Authority that would own or control all atomic energy activities and have the power to inspect. Only when such a control and inspection system was working would we stop making our bombs. Baruch gave no assurance that the United States would stop making or stockpiling atom bombs until we were satisfied at some remote and indefinite date that international control was effective. in the meantime the U.S.S.R. and others were precluded from developing atomic weapons.

Such a proposal was viewed by Russia in much the same way as we would have viewed a similar Russian proposal about intercontinental missiles. One can imagine the uproar in Congress, if after Sputnik, the Russians had indicated they would agree to stop making and testing such missiles only after an inspection system was operating and in the meantime the United States would not be free to develop space rockets or other missiles.

Six — It is said that we tried disarmament after two world wars and it failed. Actually, the Allied powers, after insisting on the disarmament of Germany, refused to disarm themselves in spite of having agreed to do so. This refusal to follow suit was one of the arguments used by German nationalists to justify German rearmament and thus put an end to the humiliating inferiority of their nation.

The Washington Naval Disarmament Conference, which resulted in the scrapping of some blueprints, and some vessels in the process of construction, after World War I, resulted in a relative increase in American naval strength rather than a decrease. The conference ended the Anglo-Japanese Treaty, thus increasing America's relative strength in the Pacific. It also resulted in a 5-5-3 ratio for building and maintaining navies, thus giving the United States, without an expensive arms race, equality with Great Britain, the leading naval power of that day, and a fixed advantage over Japan..

Following World War II, the United States had a monopoly on the atomic bomb, a navy larger than all others, what General George Marshall called a "superior" air force, and an army of more than a million men.

Those who say that the United States disarmed after two world wars are confusing demobilization with disarmament. No nation can continue indefinitely after the end of a war to maintain the degree of mobilization reached during the war. But demobilization to peacetime military levels is a far cry from total disarmament.

Seven—Another argument used against any disarmament proposal is that it is not armaments but political tensions which cause war. Such a statement implies that armaments in the possession of one nation do not inspire fear or tension in others. Yet there was a genuine rise in political tension immediately after the Russian development of nuclear weapons and again after the successful launching of Sputnik.

Professor Robert MacIver of Columbia University, in his classic *Web of Government*, wrote:

> When historians tell us that the causes of a particular war were such and such, we still do not know why the 'causes' caused the war. They might have existed without causing the war. It is often hard to distinguish between pretexts and motivations. In the last resort, the cause of institutionalized behavior is the institution that sanctions it. Every institution sets up mechanisms for its own perpetuation.

The armaments system and the armed forces of each nation are the institutions with vested interests in preparing and planning for war. The fact of similar interests in other nations provides a convenient competition.

This was evident prior to World War I, when the French general staff insisted on large loans to Russia to modernize the Russian Army and build strategic railways to the German frontier. The Russians, in turn, bribed the Paris press to support the passage of the French government's three-year conscription bill. The German general staff became convinced that delay would add to Russian strength in 1914. The Kaiser and political rulers of Germany were unable to resist the pressure of the general staff. When Austria-Hungary, under pressure from its own general staff, decided to strike Serbia after the assassination of the Archduke, general war resulted.

Eight—In a critique of disarmament appearing in the October 11, 1959, New York *Times*, former Spanish diplomat Salvador de Madariaga made the amazing statement:

> Nations do not seek armaments as they seek wealth or food or health. They consider armaments as a burden and a nuisance which they accept merely as a necessary evil. It follows that the only way to disarm would

51

be to remove the cause which makes the evil and nuisance of armaments necessary.

This statement is simply not true. Events of 1947 and 1948 right here in the United States demonstrate clearly that nations, and especially factions within nations, do indeed "seek armaments," sometimes so eagerly as to resort to dishonest means. In 1947, after the Pentagon had failed consistently since 1944 to get University Military Training, an all-out propaganda effort was begun, wrote Colonel William Neblett in *Pentagon Politics*, to convince the nation "that we were living in a state of undeclared emergency; that war with Russia was just around the corner; and that the safety of the nation was dependent upon the speedy" build-up of the military establishment. Neblett added: "I know from my own knowledge of the men who worked up the fear campaign that they do not believe what they say. Their propaganda has always had the single objective to build a hugh conscript professional military force of 10,000,000 men under the command of a professional general staff."

The same year, 1947, Field Marshal Viscount Montgomery visited Russia and, upon his return to England, informed "the British government that it would be fifteen to twenty years before Russia would be in a position to fight a major war with any chance of success — if indeed she ever wished to embark on such a course, which I doubted."

In spite of the Pentagon's 1947 campaign, Congress did not pass Universal Military Training. In March 1948, still intent on UMT, the Army handed to President Truman a false intelligence report which indicated that Russian troops were on the move and war was only a few weeks away. The President, in an emergency session of both Houses of Congress on March 17, asked for immediate passage of the Marshall Plan, the draft, and UMT. Shortly thereafter the Central Intelligence Agency properly evaluated the Army's report as false. Yet neither the President nor the Army was prepared to correct the impression of danger they had created. General Omar N. Bradley, Army chief of staff, continued until June, 1948, to tell Congress that war with Russia was a "plausible possibility."

As a result of this trumped-up war scare, Congress passed measures designed to build America's military might.

On May 14, 1949, *United States News & World Report* said. "War scares, encouraged by high officials only a few weeks ago, so alarmed the . . . U.S. public that top planners now are having to struggle hard to keep Congress from pouring more money into national defense than the Joint Chiefs of Staff regard as wise or necessary. It is proving more difficult to turn off than to turn on a war psychology."

The Army's war talk and efforts in 1947-48 to secure the adoption of UMT and a large military establishment were a cause rather than a result of tension between the United States and the Soviet Union. It is true there were political tensions in 1948 arising from the Czech *coup d'etat*, but this followed the Army's 1947 campaign by many months. Moreover, when Congress offered a seventy group air force instead of UMT, President Truman and Army leaders felt it was unnecessary, thus confirming the analysis that they did not consider the Czech coup a forerunner of war with Russia. What they wanted was permanent universal conscription and a large peacetime army.

Nine — It is suggested that genuine agreement on disarmament is possible only if there are political settlements first. There is some truth in the idea that a relaxation of tensions is evidence of good faith in pursuing disarmament negotiations. But it is foolish to suppose that all political tensions can be eliminated from the world. If we had to wait until such a day, there never would be any hope of disarmament. If, however, we achieve total disarmament, such problems as Berlin and Formosa will be more capable of solution. So long as military might is the basis of power, no government will give up what it does not have to give up. It is precisely because a solution in Berlin or Formosa would require one government to back down and would enhance the military power advantage of another that such agreements cannot be made easily under present conditions. On the other hand, an abandonment of military power would eliminate most of the sources of tension over Berlin and Formosa.

It is nonetheless obvious that some political agreements would have to be reached before disarmament can be put into effect. Red China, for example, would have to be admitted to the United Nations if she were to be a party to a disarmament agreement which provided for inspectors on Chinese soil.

While the proposal for total universal disarmament is of such utmost importance as to raise high hopes, many grave problems lie ahead —

To avoid serious economic dislocation the United States would have to plan for the radical change from an arms to a non-military economy. Until our government undertakes such a study it is clear that any disarmament proposals or negotiations on our part are mere propaganda.

The Khrushchev proposal referred to "strictly limited contingents of police, of militia" for each country to maintain internal order. Exactly what this means must be seriously explored. Does Khrushchev intend to have large police forces in Hungary, or will he rely on the Communist Party and economic factors to keep Hungary in the Soviet orbit?

The Soviet proposal also failed to deal with the question of internal subversion. Should the international community protect small underdeveloped nations from internal subversion directed by agents of a great power? If so, how can we prevent the international community from

53

being an instrument of the *status quo* designed to thwart legitimate political and social change? It may be that the international community should continue to refrain from interfering in clearly internal state matters. In this event, would the greater economic aid available during and after disarmament insure greater internal stability for nations in the process of change?

These problems and others must be squarely faced, but they are not beyond the ability of governments to solve. The immediate problem, however, is not one of solving all the details, imortant as they are. Rather it is one of insuring that our own government commit itself to the goal of total disarmament and begin serious planning and negotiating with others to achieve that goal.

The United States cannot afford to ignore or turn down the proposal for total disarmament. To do so would be an admission that the Soviet Union is the champion of peace while we want to perpetuate the war system. Our government cannot risk being branded as the nation that stood in the way of disarmament.

But beyond all this, we Americans cannot afford to perpetuate a system which could, through blunder, miscalculation, or intention, result in the destruction of civilization and the genetic distortion of the human race.

X

America Needs a Revolutionary Strategy

(*The Progressive*, April, 1960)

Since the end of World War I, the world has been caught up in a period of revolution and upheaval. One of these revolutions erupted from the growing determination of the poor and underprivileged all over the world to better their lot. Another is the Communist revolution with all that this has implied in the way of power struggle between East and West.

For many years the United States was unable to decide which revolution was more basic. Was Communism enjoying its opportunities and building its power as a result of the revolution of the underprivileged? Or were the "poor" nations revolting only because they were inspired and aided by the Communists?

Today in Asia and Africa there is a growing body of evidence that the basic revolution is one in which racial equality, national freedom, and economic opportunity are the goals. Those who guide these revolutions turn to Communism only as a last resort against an adamant West. Communism, on the other hand, in order to meet its own dynamic goal of winning the world, has to depend on penetration and taking over non-Communist revolutionary situations and movements. Is it not possible therefore that the Communist revolution is simply riding piggyback on the revolution of the poor and dispossessed?

American policy since World War I, with a few exceptions, has been one of ignoring or suppressing these revolutions. In the Twenties and early Thirties our emphasis was on seeking a world of law free from entanglements and free from war. This period has often been characterized as one of neutralism or isolationism on our part.

In the late Thirties we shifted our emphasis toward preparation for, and then actively fighting, a war to preserve the *status quo* which Germany, Italy, and Japan threatened. Since World War II we have continued in a state of war and military preparedness in order to deal with other threats, most of them from Communist countries.

The "peace" policy of the Thirties and the "war" policy of the Fifties are in reality irrational responses to the same problem of revolution. They are irrational because we have never made either a realistic attempt to assess the meaning of the revolutions confronting the world or a serious attempt to deal with revolution and its underlying situation.

We have even permitted ourselves to drift into an attitude of frightened and frantic response to crisis after crisis instead of having an overall philosophy and strategy for revolution. This lack of understanding about what is happening and our lack of strategy in turn have led to a blind determination to stop the spread of Communism even if we have to destroy civilization to do it. The development of nuclear weapons has given us the means to back up this threat of destruction.

The combination of a lack of strategy for dealing with revolution, a willingness to destroy civilization if necessary, and the ability to do so have been gathered up in one concept—deterrence. As currently used, deterrence is a broad concept. It includes:

> The containment of Communist and allied revolutionary movements by military means.

> An ever present threat of nuclear retaliation in the hope that it will pose such risks to an aggressor that he will not proceed with his aggression.

> Retaliation with nuclear weapons if an aggressor nevertheless proceeds to strike the United States or some part of the world vital to us.

The only military variation in this policy of deterrence which has been seriously discussed is the substitution of limited war for nuclear war as the instrument to enforce containment.

In this sense limited war would be fought with conventional weapons for limited objectives and generally in a limited geographical area. A war with the Soviet Union that aimed at her destruction or at rendering her impotent could not be considered limited. Some authorities believe that very small or tactical atomic weapons could be used in limited war, but this is doubtful because such weapons are almost certain to "spread the conflagration."

In any event, as Hanson Baldwin, military analyst for the *New York Times*, points out, "the first requirement for keeping a limited war limited is, ironically, the capability of extending it." Thus the threat of nuclear retaliation would be at least as strong during a limited war. Moreover, nuclear weapons might be used if the impending loss of a limited war seemed to jeopardize our global power position. Limited war therefore does not alter the over-all problem posed by the policy of deterrence.

Professor Henry Kissinger of Harvard has defined deterrence as "the attempt to keep an opponent from adopting a certain course of action by posing risks which will seem to him out of proportion to any gains to be achieved."

His definition can be simplified by recognizing that deterrence is basically a reversal of the Golden Rule: "Be prepared to do unto others what you do not want them to do unto you"—and they won't do it. Such a policy puts the accent on fear and threat as our method of dealing with other nations. The implication of "Do unto others as you would have them do unto you" is one of winning support of others by example, by fairness and justice, or in political terms by the power of attraction. I am not now raising questions of New Testament ethics but rather of the psychological orientation of our policy. Is it possible to base our security on the threat of nuclear extermination of millions of people in Europe and Asia and at the same time convince these or other millions that they are important persons whose standard of living should be raised and whose freedom we really cherish?

Another way of asking the same question is to ask whether deterrence is an effective approach to a world in revolution. Since our adoption of this policy China has gone Communist, Hungary has lost its attempt at freedom, North Viet Nam has gone Communist, and the Bagdad Pact has been destroyed by the revolution in Iraq.

A narrower definition of deterrence is based on the acknowledgement that nuclear war has become so destructive that there is no hope of victory but only the prospect of annihilation. The argument follows, then, that if no nation will consciously seek its own death, the way to prevent war is to be prepared for the kind of war that neither side dares to wage.

One difficulty with such a policy is that it assumes that wars are started by intention rather than by blunder or miscalculation. It assumes that our adversaries are ruled by rational men and that their missile-launching devices and ours are manned by persons who won't make mistakes. Again and again our own technicians have misinterpreted the radar screen with the result that bombers were sent toward Russia. Fortunately they were called back before they had reached their destination. Intercontinental missiles which take only 30 minutes to reach their destination cannot similarly be recalled.

The expectation that both Russia and America will retaliate if attacked means that our national existence and the safety of millions of people are dependent on making no blunders. There is no margin for error on either side.

Another difficulty with the concept of deterrence is that it fosters the growth of military values and constant readiness for war. Deterrence loses its force if it is merely a bluff or if the adversary believe it is a bluff. Therefore it has to be founded on a technology, a public opinion, and a political system that will assure an immediate retaliatory response to aggression.

But deterrence is not simply intended to prevent attack on the United States. It is a policy to forestall aggression anywhere. If after a warning an aggressor nevertheless proceeds on the assumption that a limited aggression is not sufficient to precipitate a nuclear war, then we must follow through or be caught bluffing. In this sense a deterrent which is not implemented ceases to be a deterrent. In such a situation a policy of deterrence narrows our courses of action not to several possibilities but to one. The decision of whether or not we commit suicide is in the hands of an enemy; any move on his part forcing us to respond invites our own destruction.

If we are to examine deterrence seriously we must do so in the light of its ultimate meaning, nuclear retaliation. In the event of a surprise attack on the United States we have these alternatives: to retaliate by destroying the enemy or not to retaliate.

If we are largely or totally destroyed our retaliation will have lost its meaning in strategic terms, for, as Kissinger has pointed out, we shall be pursuing a strategy after the political and social basis for it has already disappeared.

A policy of nuclear retaliation with the probability of civilization being destroyed and the human race genetically distorted has been justified by the slogan: "Better no world than a Communist world." This is based on at least three assumptions:

> We accept the Communist dogma that theirs is the final revolution and conclude that there is no way of ending Communism short of destroying an entire people and an entire civilization.

> We accept the nihilistic philosophy of Hitler, namely that if we do not survive in all our glory we shall pull the rest of the race down to destruction with us.

> We have our backs to the wall and have lost confidence in our ability to discover and put into effect any policy other than the one of mutual annihilation.

If, on the other hand, we should consider the alternative policy of no nuclear retaliation we would probably accept another set of assumptions:

> We will not gain anything, once destroyed, if we destroy the rest of the race.

Neither Communism nor any other system will last forever. All systems require constant change to meet changing needs. They must change or be replaced.

There are other ways than deterrence for dealing with revolution, aggression, or Communist expansion.

If the United States were to recognize that the military policy it is now pursuing is a dead end and decide to abandon it, there would be a number of alternatives or complementary policies it could pursue.

The first and obvious one is to announce our commitment to total universal disarmament along the lines already proposed by Premier Khrushchev to the United Nations. This would require serious negotiations in an effort to translate the Khrushchev proposal into reality. It would also require large scale study and planning for economic change to a peace economy.

A second approach would involve intensive negotiation for disengagement of troops and military installations from Europe, the Middle East, and the Far East, followed by neutralization of these areas, as in Austria, the problem of guarantees against aggression being turned over to the United Nations. This idea has already been endorsed in principle by Premier Khrushchev; Adam Rapacki, the Polish foreign minister; Hugh Gaitskell, the leader of the British Labor Party; and George F. Kennan, who formerly served as head of the policy planning division in the State Department.

Third, we should use our economic power to create internal stability for resistance to subversion and as a weapon of social change in Asia and Africa. It is significant that Finland and a large part of Austria were conquered and occupied by Russian troops in 1945. The internal stability of these two nations was so strong that no significant Communist movement could develop. Without such a movement and other evidence of dissatisfaction with their own government, it would have been extremely difficult to incorporate Finland and Austria into the Communist world as satellites.

Fourth, we must not underestimate the power of attraction which a nation-state would have if it became the symbol to the peoples of Africa, Asia, South America, and Europe of their hopes for freedom, equality, plenty. We should recall the attraction power of the newly-formed Soviet Union to the labor movement in Europe and America in the 1920's when the Soviet Union had practically no other power with which to defend herself except the promise of social change and a more abundant life. In that decade the labor movement in many Western countries was so ready to give the Soviet Union a chance to make good that it would not prepare for or support a war against the Soviet Union. The United

States could similarly separate the non-Communist world from the Communist and divide the peoples of the Communist world from their leaders if we were to stop backing the *status-quo* and by our actions become the symbol of hope to the common people of the world.

Fifth, in seeking by political and economic means to deal with the problems of totalitarianism and aggression, the power of world public opinion must be used to bolster agreements and frustrate invasion or conquest. In this context, we must not overlook the effectiveness of the Communist peace offensive. It is even instructive to note that the germ warfare charges against the United States in Korea were intended as psychological warfare to prevent the use of the atom bomb by the United States in Korea and elsewhere in Asia. The United States was so placed on the defensive by these charges that it could not easily have used equally horrible atomic weapons if it had been planning to do so. The revulsion of world public opinion against the United States would have created intolerable pressure. For our part, mere propaganda would not suffice. We would have to plan acts of great political and economic significance if we intended to mobilize world public opinion.

Other creative proposals have been made. For example, George Kennan in his book, *Russia, the Atom and the West,* has suggested the unilateral disarmament of Western Europe and the building of European social and economic strength as a bulwark against Communism. In the event of invasion he would advocate violent underground resistance, Sir Stephen King-Hall of England, a former Royal Navy commander, in his book, *Defense in the Nuclear Age,* advocates unilateral disarmament and reliance on non-violent resistance.

In the final analysis all policy must be based on two assumptions:

If we are interested either in national or human survival we dare not use the weapons we have created and stockpiled.

If we want to compete successfully with Communism or any other ideology, we must recognize that economic and social revolutions cannot be deterred or contained by military power. They can be dealt with only by a superior revolutionary strategy, and that strategy must seek genuinely to meet the needs of those driven to revolution.

XI

Justice, Revolution and Violence

(Reconciliation Quarterly,
Third Quarter, 1966, London, England)

The classic Greek definition of justice is "giving to every man his due." This in turn implied that men who made a greater contribution to society should be rewarded in proportion to their contribution. From a Christian perspective, it is inadequate merely to reward a man for his contribution. God's grace is available to men in proportion to their need. Emil Brunner has suggested that justice for the helpless widow, the aged cripple, and the expectant mother must involve meeting their needs.

Justice from a Christian point of view is a by-product of love, since it is the only incentive that will move men to meet the needs of the unlovely, the powerless and the sick people of this world.

From a secular or political point of view, justice is a by-product of freedom. This means that each man must be free to develop his optimal possibilities. And this means that he must be free from poverty, from authoritarian rule, from racial discrimination, from military conscription, war, and many other things that keep him from being his best self.

Unfortunately, the word "freedom" has sometimes implied license to disregard the rights of others. Societies with a concern for justice therefore have had to protect the weak from the strong and the selfish.

Unfortunately also, governments have sometimes become either instruments in the hands of a strong man or a powerful group or class. Justice, therefore, requires that the individual have rights over against the community of which he is a part, just as the individual's freedom must at some points be subordinated to the community.

Probably the best short definition of injustice is that which dehumanizes man. So justice is that which is a man's due—his birthright as a human being, or human dignity.

Poverty, for example, is injustice, for two reasons: (1) it is unnecessary in our present state of technological development, and (2) it enslaves men to their physical requirements, often torturing them with hunger and disease. In other words, it keeps them from realizing their own true worth and therefore dehumanizes them.

There is another meaning of the word "justice" which is illustrated in a story in the book of Genesis. God revealed to Abraham his intention to destroy the wicked city of Sodom. Abraham's sense of justice was disturbed, so he spoke to the Lord saying: "Shall not the judge of all the earth do right? If there are 50 righteous persons within the city will you destroy them with the wicked?" After God assured Abraham that the city would be spared for the sake of the fifty, Abraham became uncertain about his statistics and came down from 50 to 40 to 30 to 20 and finally to ten. God said he would not destroy it for the sake of the ten. When the city was actually destroyed, the innocent were given a chance to flee before the destruction was begun.

This primitive story suggests that justice involves the discriminate application of force, not indiscriminate violence. It is not so primitive an ethic as was practiced by the United States in the destruction of Hiroshima and Nagasaki, nor as practiced in Vietnam today.

Within most modern nations today it is clearly unjust to punish the innocent along with the guilty. For example, when the police arrest a criminal, they are not permitted to shoot the criminal's relatives and friends.

This Genesis story, however, goes beyond the idea of punishing only those who are guilty, to suggest that the guilty should be spared because of the righteous who shared the city with them. Here is no Niebuhrian idea that the moral men share the guilt of the immoral society, but rather there is the idea that the wicked should somehow share in the salvation due to the righteous. The idea of salvation has invaded the concept of justice so that it cannot be thought of purely in terms of punishment in proportion to guilt.

Today, partly as a result of New Testament insights and partly as a result of modern psychological insights, justice no longer depends upon punishment of the guilty. The Christian emphasis on salvation from sin is paralleled in advanced secular societies by the conviction that crime is evidence of sickness or abnormality. Therefore the criminal must be healed or rehabilitated.

Justice in New Testament terms is not simply giving a man his due in the sense that he earns punishment or reward. Christian justice is always concerned with a man's salvation — with restoring him to his true nature as a child of God.

The Marxist contribution to our discussion is the insight that justice is not simply a matter of proper individual relationships or of government protection of the law-abiding from the criminal. Social, political, and economic systems are organized, according to Marx, in the interests of a dominant group or class and necessarily result in injustice. Such a social order depends for its existence on the exploitation of human beings.

When human patience is exceeded and the grievance against the ruling group is so great that large numbers are unwilling any longer to accept their lot, revolution becomes possible. Revolution is the answer of those who despair of justice under existing conditions.

The word revolution is not to be identified with violence, but with drastic social change. There have been revolutions in human history where social change has been accomplished by those who did not use or advocate violence. On the other hand revolutions are not possible unless the existing social order is violent in its effect.

Violence can be defined in many ways. A lawyer would probably define it as the unlawful use of physical force. But such a definition would not get to the heart of the problem since law in every society is written, administered and interpreted by those who are in a position to exploit the minority, the poor, and the powerless.

A Marxist on the other hand would think of any social order other than a classless society as being inherently violent. Such a social order is possible only if the instruments of violence such as the courts, the police, and the army are used to maintain the position and privileges of the ruling class. This Communist identification of the classless society with social peace is in some respects parallel to the Old Testament idea of peace *(shalom)*, which means that the goal of God (or history) for men has been realized in a community of righteousness, mercy, and truth. The difficulty with this Marxist idea is its assumption that by definition Communism is the historical goal through which peace and harmony and justice will be achieved. The truth in the analysis is its identification of the structure of society with violence.

The Christian pacifist tends to accept the truth in the Marxist analysis while recognizing that no perfect social order is possible in the sense that it will produce perfect justice or men free from sin. On the other hand, pacifists and Marxists both believe that the structure of society can be changed so as to eliminate organized violence in the form of war.

The pacifist might define violence as the social or individual use of power in a non-redemptive way so as to injure persons or harm their welfare.

It is not impossible of course to deepen both the Marxist and the pacifist understanding of violence. For example, in a recent visit to Prague I had a two-hour conversation with a leading Marxist about the Christian-Communist dialogue taking place there. He rejected the idea that such dialogue could be a tactic to convert the opponent or to take advantage of him. He said, "Dialogue is incompatible with the use of violence or the use of power against the dialogue partner because it destroys the possibility of real honest discussion. Dialogue is very important to the whole human enterprise because it is the only way to inner development."

This, he acknowledged, "is a deepening of Marxist insight to find that there are areas of life incompatible with violence."

The pacifist, on the other hand, must acknowledge far more than he does the violence in the existing social order. In America, for example, during the civil rights campaign a few pacificsts were very critical of Negroes whose demonstrations or boycotts disturbed the life of the community. Actually, American society has inflicted upon Negroes injustice in the form of poverty, racial segregation, police brutality, and inadequate education, so that in desperation they demonstrate. Even if some Negroes do not stick to the rules of non-violence, why should we assume that they are creating the violence? The heart of the problem is that the economic and social order in which Negroes live was built up by violence and is maintained by violence.

Earlier I suggested that revolution is not to be identified with the use of violence. Now we should add that it is not to be confused with the overthrow of a particular government. A change in government or a shift from one ruling group to another does not necessarily involve the ending of injustice. The American Civil War of 1860-64 was not a revolution, even though it resulted in the ending of human slavery in the United States. It was no longer legally possible to own slaves. But the Southern white man and many in the North continued to treat Negroes as if they were still a form of property to be exploited. It was this continued degradation of persons that has produced the current non-violent racial revolution in the United States one hundred years after the Civil War of 1860. Revolution implies a new political, social, or economic beginning — the elimination of an old and unjust order and the birth of a new order.

This means that the test of whether an event is revolutionary is not in the intention of those who set it in motion, but the end result — if it has in fact turned things upside down and accomplished creative social change. This is to say that the intentions of men are insufficient. It is the meaning of the event as given by God or history.

It is possible, for example, to say that the so-called Hungarian Revolution of 1956 or the rebellion in Germany of soldiers and workers in 1919 or the 1905 revolt in Russia or the Peasants Revolt in Luther's day were not revolutions because they offered no new beginning. But it is not possible to speak in the same way about the Russian Revolution which created the Soviet Union or the Gandhian non-violent struggle which signalled the ending of colonialism. They did create a new beginning and a new order.

There is a sense in which Christianity is anti-revolutionary. It assumes that the only new beginning in history was the unique intervention of God in Jesus Christ. All else that happens is either renewal or the effort to call individuals to change in the direction of Christian obedience. Those who hold to this often believe that Christians should stay out of politics or racial movements and confine their activity to the church. Specifically in terms of racial justice they would argue that the church should witness to society by its own racial inclusiveness, not by trying actively to promote racial justice in the secular world.

Over against this is the idea that the church exists to work in society to change the established order into an order of freedom and justice. "This," said Professor Jacques Ellul at the Amsterdam Assembly, "is a mission of 'permanent revolution.'"

Permanent revolution from the Christian perspective means that every order which falls short of the standards of God is unstable and carries within it the seeds of its own destruction. But it also means that Christians must be active in exposing the injustice of the existing order and in encouraging the birth of a new order. Those who preach love in our kind of society can purchase immunity from conflict only at the price of hypocrisy.

Christians must therefore see that the upheavals of our time brought about by the violence and injustice of the social order are indications that changes are demanded by God. These upheavals point to the new order which God wills for men but which is not fully revealed.

We cannot, however, say that the church or Christianity is the inspirer of revolution. Often it has been the conservative influence that tried to maintain the *status quo*. Neither can we say that Karl Marx and the Russian Revolution provide the great inspiration for modern revolution. There is a sense in which the affluence of America is as much an incentive to revolution as the Communism of Russia. Because of modern technology which has so dominated American life, it is now possible for every society to think of eradicating poverty. This is another way of saying that the privileged group which has a vested interest in preserving its own special privilege often provides the incentive for revolution.

In every revolutionary situation there is always the problem of power. The power of the dispossessed must be exerted against the power of the established order. Because power is often associated with the ability to use violence, revolutions have often tended to be violent.

Power has often been defined as the ability to achieve purpose. It is now known that there are many ways of achieving purpose, ranging all the way from persuasion to coercion. Coercion can be moral, political, military, or manifest in still other forms.

Basically the problem for every revolution is what is the most appropriate power for the ending of injustice and the bringing in of the new order.

There are at least four reasons for rejecting violence as a method of revolution today:

(1) The established order has a monopoly on the major weapons of violence. Any armed group that uses violence against a modern military force is always in danger of retributive genocide. This is evident in Vietnam today. The Vietnamese National Liberation Front want to seize power from the South Vietnamese government and the American invaders, whereas the chief strategy of the American military is to make the guerrilla revolution so costly by mass killing that the Communists will abandon it as a method. If both sides persist in the present struggle for another five or ten years, there is real danger of genocide.

(2) Violent revolution implies the willingness to destroy everything of the older order. Violence is not necessarily concerned with preserving the values of the former system. Non-violence is the only way to conserve the values of the past while bringing in a new order.

(3) The modern revolutionary purpose is negated by violence. The revolutionary purpose holds that human life is more important than possessions or power or anything else. All politics and all economics should be directed towards helping men and women find their highest good. Yet violent revolution asserts that the aims of the revolution are more important than the persons it is designed to benefit.

(4) If the revolution is intended to eliminate the violence and injustice implicit in the social order, it can do so only by providing a non-violent alternative structure for fulfilling the necessary functions of the old social structure. It is unlikely that a revolutionary movement based on violence will, at the peak of violent power, renounce the instruments that brought them to power. The maintenance of the instruments of violence by any ruling group presupposes their use against another group.

If violence is rejected, one has to do it either from an idealistic or a pragmatic approach. Christian pacifists have tended to be almost wholly idealistic or Biblically obedient in their rejection of violence.

In Prague in my discussions with Marxists I raised the question of non-violence. The response was: "If to attain a particular goal non-violence is the best possible way, then it is not incompatible with Marxism. But non-violence in the Christian or Gandhian sense is much more than this and transcends the pragmatic." After stating why he thought a Marxist approach provided a "deeper analysis of the real dynamics of the present situation" and a way for "the shaping of the optimal possibilities of persons, society and the world" he said, "For this reason I have no need for non-violence as a programme. I have a high regard for Gandhi, and Jesus, but they are unnecessary."

This contrast betwen the pragmatic and idealist conceptions of non-violence is too easily asserted by both Christians and Marxists.

Both in India and in America in the course of the non-violence struggles there were those who engaged in non-violence solely for pragmatic reasons. It is significant however that it was Gandhi and not Nehru who provided the leadership, just as in America, Martin Luther King rather than certain other figures became the symbol of the freedom campaign. This is to say that the combination of the idealist and the pragmatist in one person and in a movement has more power than either approach by itself.

The reason this is so is found first in the very nature of power. The ability of any ruler or ruling group to rule depends upon the cooperation and obedience of the people. There must always be the consent of the governed. Gandhi put it this way:

"At the back of the policy of terrorism is the assumption that terrorism if applied in a sufficient measure will produce the desired result, namely, bend the adversary to the tyrant's will. But supposing a people make up their mind that they will never do the tyrant's will . . ."[1]

In any given situation there must be not only an understanding of the dynamics of power but a faith that transcends and gives meaning to the sufferings of those who non-violently resist tyranny. Just as violence feeds on hatred, so non-violence must depend on the impact that suffering without retaliation makes on both the active user of violence and on the passive spectator.

"We're going to win our freedom," a Negro leader said at a mass meeting in Birmingham last year, "and as we do it we're going to set our white brothers free." A short while later, when the Negroes faced a barricade of police dogs, clubs, and fire hoses, they "became spiritually intoxicated," as another leader described it. "This was sensed by the police and firemen and it began to have an effect on them. I don't know what happened to me. I got up from my knees and said to the cops, 'We're not turning back. We haven't done anything wrong. All we want is our freedom. How do you feel doing these things?' The Negroes started advancing and Bull Connor shouted: 'Turn on the water!' But the firemen did not respond. Again he gave the order and nothing happened. Some observers claim they saw firemen crying. Whatever happened the Negroes went through the lines. The next day Bull Connor was reported

[1] Gandhi, *Non-Violence in Peace and War,* Vol. I, p. 174.

by the press to have said, 'I didn't want to mess their Sunday clothes, all those people from church."[2]

The phrase "Non-violence" can be defined as organized, disciplined, direct action against injustice or aggression in such a way as to demonstrate respect for the personality of opponents while seeking to end the injustice they are inflicting or perpetuating. Non-violence generally involves some form of non-cooperation with evil such as a boycott, strike, sit-in, mass demonstration. Such non-cooperation is generally made as dramtic and open as possible so as to tell the truth to the world as to the way the non-violent resisters feel about the evil inflicted upon them.

"Non-violence" is therefore a combination of the social and economic power of non-cooperation with the moral power of voluntary suffering for others. It assumes (1) that there is power in withdrawing support from evil or exploiting institutions; (2) that opponents are human beings like ourselves, to be respected and not violated; and (3) that the acceptance of suffering rather than inflicting it on others is itself a form of power, demoralizing to those who use violence without experiencing it in return, and troublesome to the conscience of those who are not directly involved in the struggle.

The spirit of non-violence is apparent in Martin Luther King's statement: "We have no desire to triumph over the white man and we seek no such victory. When segregation on the buses is ended, this will not be a victory for the Negro over the white man, but of justice over injustice. And it will be a victory for the best interests of the white people as well."

Some of the advantages of the non-violent approach are:

(1) It is a method for fighting injustice which the physically weak as well as the strong may use since it does not depend on physical but upon other types of force.

(2) It is a method which does not antagonize but tends to win a neutral or a "moderate" group not completely committed to either side.

(3) It tends to divide rather than unite opponents because of such factors as elimination of fear of violence from the mind of the opponents, dislike of seeing people suffer heroically without inflicting suffering in return, or a conscious or subconscious feeling that those using non-violent action have a sympathetic understanding of their opponents' position.

(4) It does not indulge in the excesses which accompany violence and thus distract from the original goals. Rather, it focuses attention steadily and sharply on the injustice.

---

[2] Dave Dellinger, *The Future of Non-Violence*, Gandhi Marg, July, 1965.

(5) It builds up in the opponent surprise, reassurance, then respect and understanding, and eventually a feeling of kinship or unity.

(6) Non-violence spurs the group using it to self-improvement. Violence aims at subduing the opponent and all is focused on the enemy, whereas non-violence turns the searchlight inward. In Montgomery, during the bus boycott, although more Negroes were driving cars, the accident rate and violations of traffic laws dropped, and there were fewer crimes of violence on the part of Negroes. Their leaders said, "Sometimes we have been accused of being dirty. Let us make certain by our cleanliness that there is no basis in fact for this." In other ways they focused on self-improvement. Non-violence therefore involves the development of a constructive programme that goes way beyond the resistance to oppression.

In India, you may recall, the spinning wheel was symbolic of the drive to get Indians to begin the development of self-help programmes, a vital part of their non-violent movement.

The problems of justice, revolution and violence will not of course be resolved by discussions in closed circles. The successful use of non-violent revolutionary force, as in India and the United States, make the greatest contribution. Another important contribution to the resolution of these problems is in the dialogue between Marxists and Christians, especially Christian pacifists.

The dialogue has been immeasurably aided by the whole revolution in warfare. That military revolution includes the following:

(1) The development of a variety of expensive and complex weapons so that the state alone has a monopoly of such weapons. It is this fact that produced such a disparity of power between Russian tanks and Hungarian rifles in the abortive Hungarian revolution.

(2) The development of nuclear weapons, which creates the risk that any conventional warfare may escalate into world destruction.

(3) In turn this danger of escalation and this monopoly of the weapons of mass destruction have led the Communist world to think in terms of guerrilla warfare as a method of national revolution.

(4) The success of the method of guerrilla warfare in China, Algeria, Cuba, and French Indo-China has led the American military to decide on a strategy for dealing with guerrilla war. That strategy, which is unfolding in Vietnam, is the use of weapons of mass destruction to make guerrilla warfare too costly for the Communists to pursue. An American General was quoted in the 15th May, 1966, *New York Times* as saying, "The French didn't kill enough. If you kill enough you win the war." The *New York Times* in comment said, "The proposition that a solution to the Vietnam war can somehow be found if the United States

and the Saigon government can kill enough Vietnamese Communists has remained one of the basic elements in American policy."

When I was in Prague in May, 1966, I visited the National Liberation Front office. In the course of a five-hour discussion I raised the question of non-violent resistance as a better way of securing national liberation. I pointed out that there were two dangers in the present course:

(a) The Pentagon is prepared for a long war with no thought of withdrawal. It does not need to win in the traditional sense; it needs only to destroy on such a scale as to make stalemate or even ultimate victory for the NLF worse than defeat. In Vietnam even without war forty percent of the children die before the age of four, so that genocide is a practical possibility.

(b) There was also the possibility of further escalation into a nuclear third world war. When the U.S. armed forces suffer serious reverses, their only answer is to escalate the war. There are only four places to escalate — the invasion of Cambodia, the bombing of Hanoi, and the bombing of Haiphong, and war with China. This means that guerrilla warfare involving Communists is a part of the world power struggle and calculations must be made by both sides in terms of the risk of nuclear war.

In the course of the conversation at the NLF office it became apparent that there was a complete misunderstanding of non-violence, in spite of the fact that the Buddhist priests had on two occasions used non-violence techniques in the middle of war to cause the downfall of the Diem government and to force Premier Ky to promise elections. One task we have, therefore, is to educate as to the meaning of non-violent struggle. Another task is to interpret the necessity for it.

In more sophisticated Communist circles in the Western world the dialogue task includes discussing other factors, such as the nature of men, the nature of power, the divorcing of certain Gandhian practices such as fasting and an emphasis on rural industry from the essence of non-violence, and the divorcing of certain Christian ideas that non-violence is the abstention from violence rather than an active method of revolutionary change.

We must recognize that Marxism is an effort to combine the idealistic with the pragmatic and that a Christianity which does not seek to apply Biblical insights to the problems of injustice, revolution, and violence in a practical way will always be on the defensive in our world. After all, man's alienation from God is in part a by-product of his alienation from his own social order. The underdeveloped world lacks the technology with which to eliminate poverty and the developed world has created a technology whose chief use is preparation for war and preservation of privilege.

The task of dialogue must be pursued with our fellow Christians as well as with Eastern and Western Marxists. We must, for example, come to grips with the question whether non-violence as a political strategy is derived from our understanding of the New Testament as Gandhi suggested or whether Niebuhr is right that the cross cannot be interpreted stratigically.

It is certainly clear that the gospel does not provide us with a political position which could be organized into a Christian political party. The Kingdom of God rests in judgement on all political and economic systems. But the question still remains as to whether the gospel does not suggest a method for dealing with conflict as well as a responsibility for constructive social change. In other words non-violence is not synonymous with our Christian faith, but is consonant with the spirit of love.

Non-violence is not uniquely Christian since it has been and often is used by non-Christians. But it may be that it is a secularized version of Christian approach to conflict which can and must be used in our contemporary world.

XII

Christian Dynamic for Social Change

(Chapter from The Word of God in The Nuclear Age,
Church Peace Mission, 1959)

I. THE QUESTION OF RELEVANCE

A discussion of social change and of what is relevant either in the immediate scene or to the wider history of the race should be begun with the utmost humility. It would be difficult even for the most positive of Christians to dismiss views other than his own as having no relationship to the immediate or the ultimate course of events. God has not only set truth in the midst of paradox so that the foolish things of the world confound the wise, and the weak things confound the mighty, but He also has a way of taking the mistakes and foibles of men and weaving them into a large pattern of meaning and purpose.

This does not, of course, absolve us of responsibility to make our words and works have as much relationship to the kind of society we seek as does the scientist in his work with cause and effect. Nor should it keep us from being critical of programs that seem to be illusory. But it does serve as a caution in a day when as Rutenber puts it, "the lust for relevance" dominates so much of ethical thinking.

In beginning this discussion we must not assume that the evil in "immoral society" or in the situation is so great that anything relevant must be a compromise with the evil in an effort to relate ourselves to it. On the contrary it is valid to assume that goodness has its power of immediate attraction and that in a universe created and ruled by a good God, goodness is ultimately more relevant than evil.

At the outset also it is well to suggest that the relevance of any program or strategy is not determined by its potential or actual popularity with large groups of people. Pluralities and even majorities have been known to be wrong in their analysis of events as well as in their proposals for solving problems.

Rather, relevance is determined by the pertinence of the program to the problem that requires solution.

Not everyone who takes a pacifist position is concerned about relevance. There are some who believe they are called to a personal or group witness against war. Like the early Christians whose concern was to be related to the Kingdom of God rather than one of relevance to the political struggles of this world, their witness may nonetheless have political implications which history may deem more relevant than those of us who seek to be relevant.

However, those who do engage in politcal and social action necessarily must analyze the situation confronting them and develop a strategy for dealing with it.

II. THE WORLD SCENE

In one sense the present world situation can be described as a power struggle between two great political blocs. But in another sense the problem we face is a culmination of generations of inability to deal with the problem of social change. Certainly the present world situation has its roots deep in revolution.

A. The Problem of Communism

One of the three great problems which is troubling the non-communist world today — Communism — is, according to Toynbee, a revolt against Western culture. When the Soviet revolution started, it was launched against capitalism, the economic system of the West, and imperialism, which was the Western system of exploiting or colonizing non-capitalist areas. It was originally anti-war since it viewed war as a part of capitalist and Western culture. It likewise opposed religion which seemed so integral to Western culture. It also rejected Western political and juridical systems. The one aspect of Western culture it was prepared immediately to adopt and use was technology. Later it developed a war machine comparable to those in the West.

In its essence today communism and communist nations are still enaged in revolt against the West even though the revolt has taken on much of the character of a power struggle. The Soviet peace offensive, accompanied by proposals for disarmament or withdrawals of troops or comparable political moves, are not an indication of a willingness to abandon revolution but rather signal a temporary shift in strategy.

The struggle over Germany is not over, as the Berlin crisis attests. Communist parties still encourage and in some areas are seeking to lead revolts against Western imperialism. And the Communist pressures southward and eastward in Asia are continuing.

B. Revolutionary Movements

The second great problem confronting the world is what Walter Lippman in 1955 called "an epidemic of revolutionary movements, some of them overt and some still latent, in large parts of Asia, Africa, and Latin

America." He added that "they would happen even if Moscow said nothing and did nothing about them." This revolution is also in large part anti-American and anti-European in that it is a revolt against 300 years of Western imperialism, economic inequality, and racism. We are not only in the position of reaping what we have sown, but we as Westerners are among the upper classes of a world which is now caught in what Marxists call the class struggle. Millions of people throughout the world see in us their exploiters who must be overthrown or otherwise rendered powerless to exploit.

C. The Revolution in War

The third great problem confronting the world is the scientific and technological revolution that has also led to a revolution in the weapons and strategy of war, as well as changing drastically our concepts of time and space. War has ceased to be the servant of nations. It is now clearly the master, holding the power to destroy human life on the planet. None but the most sanguine believes that there is plenty of time in which to solve the problem of war.

In one sense the Communist peace offensive is simply a Soviet strategy of cold war, but in another sense it is the recognition by the Soviet Union that in the hearts of people the revolution against war has begun and they must manipulate it.

The mood of the day is one of urgency; the need is for drastic social change; discontent is widespread. Yet many American Christians have been so preoccupied with the prosperity and apparent reliability of the American structure that their net influence is one of discouraging social change, encouraging military containment of both communist and noncommunist revolutionary movements, and support of a diabolical military system.

D. The Complexity of Evil in the World

The political scene, however, is not something amoral which can be examined apart from ethical and theological considerations. The evil we see in war, in imperialism or racism, for example, is not simply the result of mistakes on the part of presidents or foreign ministers. If the international evils we have been discussing were the result of misguidance, an appeal to reason might correct them. On the contrary, there are powerful, deep-rooted vested interests which profit economically or gain status and prestige from the maintenance of the war system, imperialism, or the myths of racial inequality.

It is one thing to recognize the explosive nature of the present world scene. It is another and far more difficult task to suggest what Christians might or should do about it.

The very immensity and complexity of the evil in our world leads to the conclusion that there is no possibility of saving the present civili-

74

zation by some slight or easy amelioration or by some political formula or accommodation of interests. Rather we must recognize the sin in ourselves as well as in our opponents and emphasize the need for repentance on the part of the individual, the Church and the nation as a precondition for God's operating through us.

III. CHRISTIAN ETHICS AND SOCIAL CHANGES

If repentance is the pre-condition for creative change, our political action ought to be guided by Christian ethics rather than by simple political expediency, however important political solutions will be. Certainly we cannot be guided either by a desire to avoid trouble or by bold calculated risks designed to save what we have.

A. The Christian's first responsibility is to God. This suggests not only that the Christian should joyously seek a close Father-Son relationship with God but that he should seek in his relationship with his fellow men the kind of relationship he wants with God.

B. Such a relationship is possible only on the basis of respect for personality. This means recognizing the intrinsic value of each person so that he is not a tool to be used, exploited, or humiliated. The Fatherhood of God thus implies a brotherhood of men in which I seek for my brother the same rights I want for myself. "Whatsoever ye would that men should do to you, do ye even so to them."

C. The Christian therefore has social responsibility. This means that the Christian should consciously encourage the development of a society where personality is respected, where man's welfare is a primary concern of the community and where man's growth is fostered as the result of a process of participation in decision making.

D. The Christian's social responsibility is not parochial but ecumenical. It extends to men in other lands as well as those in our own. In spite of division and difference we are biologically and psychologically one race in need of functioning as an interdependent whole.

E. The teaching of love is so central to Christianity and so radical in its demands (love even of enemies) that a complete yielding to it would involve the acceptance of suffering upon oneself rather than the inflicting of suffering upon others. The cross is clear evidence that obedience to God and living the life of love do not necessarily bring immediate social gains. Love may not therefore be viewed as a technique or simple strategy for social change. Nor is immediate success the major criterion for Christian action. Rather God calls the Christian to live a life of love, overcoming evil with good.

F. In confronting the fact of evil, including injustice, inequality, the power some men use to dominate other men, the prejudices arising from difference, the vested political and economic interests, the Christian is constrained to act as fully as he can in the spirit of love, for the greatest

75

good, choosing the best possible method or course of action open to him. This suggests that any course of action motivated by hatred, vindictiveness, envy, or self or national aggrandizement is out of harmony with the spirit of love and the goal of the greatest good. It also implies that Christians should not be content with a lesser of two evils but with the least evil and therefore the best possible.

G. In seeking the greatest good in a complex society, justice has become a major aim of Christian ethics. Justice presupposes the subordination of man's private interest to the social group and in turn the recognition by the group that each man has rights essential to human dignity. Where man's rights to freedom, equality, and a decent life are denied, the seeds of revolution are present. As Walter Muelder suggests, "The right of revolution is inherent in the dignity of man and the system of moral law."

H. But if revolution is to serve the common good and not be simply another means of negating justice or infringing human rights, the question of how revolution is to be accomplished or how social change is to be effected becomes crucial. In a large sense, the same question is involved in confronting modern war with its potential both for destroying civilization and for genetic distortion of the human race.

I. The record of history indicates that violence is not essential to revolution or social change. The largely unplanned Industrial Revolution was not revolution of armed violence. The achievement of freedom for slaves in Great Britain was one of the unplanned social results of.the Wesleyan Reformation. The Gandhian revolution against colonialism in India was consciously non-violent. It was effective in India and far-reaching in its impact on other parts of the world.

J. Man's social nature is not basically violent, however frequently in history political groups have resorted to military means.

Man has not only developed non-violent techniques for social change; he has sought to institutionalize them in what we call government. The formal concentration of coercive power in government, whatever else may be said about it, is intended to maintain an order or coordination in society that removes disputes from the realm of military struggle.

Yet, as Robert McIver points out, force is not the real cement of government. ". . . in the family, the primary social unit, there are always present the curbs and controls that constitute the essence of government." Government he adds "is the continuation by the more inclusive society of a process of regulation that is already highly developed within the family." *(The Web of Government, p.p. 22-23)*

Wars in our complex society are possible not because men largely seek to slay their fellows but because military processes have been identified with the preservation of a national community against external

76

foes who would enslave or destroy it. The military institution is of course much more deeply embedded in the economic, social and political life of a people than this by itself implies. And it has been as frequently used for aggression as for so-called defense. Yet man's social nature is so far from being a basically violent one that men have to be conscripted, or induced with rewards, to become a part of the armed forces. And as the competent study, *Men Against Fire*, by Brig. Gen. S. L. A. Marshall reveals, combat trained men, under orders in time of war do not easily kill enemy human beings. Large percentages actually avoid shooting at specific human targets.

IV. POSSIBILITIES FOR CHRISTIAN ACTION

If Christians confront the present world scene in the spirit of love seeking the best possible course consistent with respect for human personality and the achievement of justice, they have to ask what courses of action may or may not be open to them.

A. The Problem of Aggression

For example, could Christians maintain that the best possible way to deal with an aggressor in the spirit of love is massively to retaliate with nuclear bombs probably inducing further retaliation from the enemy? I think not, for Christians would then be responsible for destroying millions of their brothers, leveling civilizations, and for genetic damage to the human race.

If Christians hold that submission to aggression is the only alternative to massive retaliation, they would, I think, fall into the Niebuhrian over-simplification of World War II which suggested that Christians were confronted with only two evil choices, submission to Nazi tyranny or support of war.

There are other conceivable choices, such as:

1. The development of a dynamic diplomacy which can through negotiation and other methods remove the major causes of Soviet-American tension, including the threat of war.

2. Non-violent defense such as that suggested by Sir Stephen King Hall in *Defense in the Nuclear Age.*

3. Launching a non-violent movement for drastic social change on a world wide scale that would tend to make people withdraw their support from any government that sought by violence to oppose such change.

4. Making our own society so attractive to other peoples that they will, through what George Kennan calls the power of attraction, want to model their own country after ours and will exert every effort to keep any aggressor from seeking to destroy a society which has become to them one of hope.

B. The Problem of Defeat or Conquest

If Christians live in a nation that has experienced defeat and conquest, there may still be a number of courses open other than simply submission.

1. When Rome, an aggressor in its day, conquered the two countries with the highest culture of the time, Greece and Israel, the Greeks and Hebrews filled the vacuum in Rome and Greek art, science and philosophy and the Hebrews with religion thus radically changing the nature of Rome. A vacuum in another country, however, can be filled only with a superior cultural contribution at one or more points.

2. Non-violent resistance coupled with attempts to win the invader may be a method for reasserting independence. If Hungary, for example, instead of using violence on Russian troops or implying that it might line up with a rival Western bloc, had used non-violence, that nation might today have at least as much freedom as Poland has. Instead of ending their revolution, as they did after they were defeated by arms, with a general strike marked by great bitterness, they might have begun with one as a temporary device to dramatize their grievances to the Russians as well as to the world. If in addition they had shown genuine friendship to Russian troops, seeking by personal contact to win them to a sympathetic understanding of their demands, their struggle could have been (a) one in which no violent threat to Russia was posed, (b) one which would have dramatized their case before world public opinion, (c) a longer-lasting struggle and hence one of longer-term pressure on the Soviet Union, (d) and one which posed risks to occupying armies in the way of disgruntled troops, defections, or desertions, and troops who would carry a different story than the official one when they returned home.

3. Non-violent campaigns for eliminating specific injustices or inequalities such as the method used by the Negro churches in Montgomery, Alabama, might be either the best that could be done immediately following defeat or might in any event be a preliminary approach to a fuller struggle for freedom later.

C. Influencing National Policy in Peacetime

Although many Christians have believed there are courses short of war open to their nation for the solution of international tension, they have also tended to believe these essentially non-violent solutions can be pursued while the nation is also devoting its energies and its diplomacy to an arms race. It is difficult, for example, at one and the same time to concede the necessity of a military struggle and to deny the nation access to alliances, military aid programs, and military bases in other nations which the military chiefs of staff say are essential to that military struggle. It is even more difficult, and, I think, impossible, for a nation to do what its military staffs demand and at the same time aid independence movements in the colonies of countries allied to our nation, to aid people in achieving economic and political freedom when they are controlled by army dictatorships receiving military aid from our military budget, etc. It is quite as difficult or impossible to help countries advance from feudalism when the feudal interests are financed by huge oil companies whose interests are protected by military diplomacy that fears that any change may open the floodgates to communism.

Those who find themselves in this dilemma are in effect caught in the position of supporting two mutually contradictory policies at the same time. To some degree they are functioning on the assumption that it is possible to propose and work for a program that will end the war system and the vested interests connected with it and at the same time be acceptable to those who support war and profit from the war system.

One difficulty with this advocacy of social change within the context of maintenance of the war system is that social change, if it takes place at all, takes place too slowly and is encourged only if it advances the purposes of the war system or the power position of the nation.

It would be a mistake for Christians to assume that power states, deriving their present power from military might, and military alliances with foreign governments in whom they have confidence, will willingly give up armaments even by agreement or will work to encourage social change at crucial points around the world. As Dorothy Fosdick, who formerly served on the State Departments Policy Planning Staff, suggests in her book *Common Sense and World Affairs,* "Many persons in official and important quarters, far from wanting to search for any system for the international control and reduction of armaments and armed forces, which would safeguard the security of every nation, are 'scared to death' of the idea. They are actually afraid the Soviet Union might sometime get 'sincere,' and hope against hope she won't."

Is it not probable that these officials will begin seriously to negotiate for universal disarmament only if forced to do so as an alternative to seeing a significant movement for unilateral disarmament grow in the United States?

Is it not probable that governments will permit or encourage social change more as a result of the pressures of those who are prepared to go all out for it by abandoning armaments than as a result of the moderate suggestions of those who support a military system that is the very antithesis of social change?

The fact that such a strategy coincides with the necessities of the nuclear age is not without significance. In *The Divine Imperative,* Emil Brunner notes the relevance of unilateral disarmament by writing that "war has now become a method which cannot any longer be reckoned as an item in any political reckoning of gain or loss. The idea of 'winning' a war . . . no longer has any place in reality . . . Therefore, if a nation were to disarm, and render itself 'defenseless'— in the old sense of the word — in order to prepare the way for the new form of 'security,' such action would not be a sign of political folly but of political wisdom, since it would demonstrate the possibility of a new way of political action."

If it be argued that if it is folly to advocate a course of action that government officials will not take, it would be well to examine the question of what action is relevant.

D. Relevance and the Nature of Government

The question of relevance is bound up with our analysis of authority and government.

Relevance is not determined simply by access to those who hold formal authority. Too often the average citizen thinks that if he had direct access to the President or Congress and could present effectively the case for world disarmament or world government or some other panacea, something useful would be accomplished.

And sometimes minorities think that they can become relevant and alter the course of events by peripheral action or by joining and compromising with the majority who support war rather than by changing the major premise to which society is committed. Such reasoning misses the point.

In the final analysis the question of political relevance is bound up with our analysis of authority and government. Government is the administrative organ of the state. Government, either in its totalitarian or democratic form, is not the complete and final authority. Government did not create society. It is society that created and sustains government. Society is made up of many social relationships such as the family, church, business, labor, community relationships, etc. Involved in these relationships are many powerful factors such as customs, traditions, status, and property.

How ever much government may be an instrument of force and coercion, it would be a mistake to think that government was created by or sustained by the ability of a group of men to exercise force over the people who are to be governed.

The power of government is simply the formal expression of the authority of the other social relationships that sustain it. Another way of saying this is that the laws and actions of a government do not necessarily express the real will of the men who serve as the executives and legislators in government. A majority of persons in the House of Representatives, for example, were individually for U.M.T. in 1952 when they voted to defeat it. They nevertheless had to adjust to the pressures of public opinion as reflected by the churches, the schools, labor, farm, and other groups. Similarly, in Tito's Yugoslavia, the government, although formally supreme, could not impose a land collectivization program against the real will of the farmers.

As Prof. Robert MacIver puts it, "All the components of social power impinge on government, diverting its formal superiority to the service of their own ends. Since these ends are in conflict one with another, there is nearly always struggle and often division of counsel within the governing body itself."

E. The Role of the Church

Let us take the church as an example. Is it more relevant to try to persuade Congress to abandon war or to persuade the Church to do so? In some respects the church is the most powerful institution in our society. All other social groups cultivate the church because to some extent they cannot act without some claim to moral justification. Business seeks the support of the church for the free enterprise system; labor and its friends have supported a Religion and Labor Foundation or used clergymen as chaplains in unions. The Army, Navy, and Air Force rely on chaplains to soften the moral impact of killing on the soldier and to give religious sanction to war.

When it comes to war, the nation cannot go to war without some claim to moral justification. In large part this is the reason for blaming aggression on the other nation or for calling our own action a "police action" in the interests of world order. All too often today the power struggle between Russia and America is viewed as a struggle between atheistic Communism and Christian civilization.

The church is indispensable to war, either as an active or silent partner. This was true in America; it was true in Germany; it was true in Russia; it was true in all nations during World War I and World War II.

With the full and active disapproval of the church, war would be extremely unlikely if not impossible. Nothing would have a greater impact on the institution of war and militarism in our own country than the active opposition of the Christian church which had itself decided to reject war. If the Christian Church* in this land were to reject war and commit itself unceasingly to the peacemaker role Jesus called blessed, the impact on the church in other lands would also be revolutionary. Christians elsewhere would know that they could count upon American Christians to wage war on war, not to wage war on their brothers

---

*Note: References to the church are not to the entire church membership but to what we might call the inner church or the vocal minority of clergy and laymen who constitute the social action movements, the leadership in women's societies, the professors in schools of theology, church governing bodies, etc.

in other lands. The missionary movement would not be suspect as agents of American imperialism.

The world Church could not turn a deaf ear to an American Church that was truly ecumenical. For our part, we could do more to oppose militarism and war-making in other lands by encouraging the church in all lands to reject war than we could by any other process.

Those who believe that it is easier to persuade all of society or government itself to abandon war than it is to persuade the church are, I think, unrealistic. The church has vested interests, but not to the same extent that government has. The church has at least a verbal commitment to Jesus' way of love that other social groups and government do not have. Its music, its scriptures, and its symbolism are friendly to pacifism and not to war. In what other groups do we find thousands of leaders committed to pacifism as we do in the Church.

Unless one or more of the real sources of authority exert influence upon government, it is obvious that a minority of pacifists cannot by writing letters, lobbying, or other legislative activity win government to accept one or more pacifist proposals. A change of law or procedure by government must therefore be preceded by more fundamental changes on the part of people and institutions. This does not mean that a minority of pacifists cannot influence government. But their influence is more likely to come as a result of non-cooperation with evil or a dramatic demonstration of moral action than by a written or verbal appeal to the President or Congress. The refusal of Quakers and Jehovah's Witnesses to cooperate with unjust laws has influenced governments partly because other groups took up the fight as a result of disturbed conscience and partly because the suffering for principle created administrative and political problems.

Thus, any action which changes the theological climate and hence the mood of the church will be felt politically. And any action which touches the moral or economic nerve of farmers, labor, or others will have political implications.

Utopian solutions are irrelevant precisely because they seek a future goal which has no rootage in immediate action. World government is utopian and irrelevant if it remains in the realm of hope and talk. But the minute the individual Christian (or the church) begins to live and act like a world citizen, he is a political factor to be reckoned with in a nationalist society.

Similarly, advocacy of universal disarmament is utopian if its achievement is dependent upon action taken by a rival nation. But when disarmament of your own nation begins with disarmed individuals and a disarmed church, then governments on both sides must take political note.

Moral power is the power that comes through individual or group commitment to principle to such an extent that they are willing to suffer for it. Such power is politically relevant even though unintended as a political strategy because it disturbs people and governments from their complacency and forces them either to choose social change or to inflict suffering. Such a choice is very difficult for governments because the inflicting of suffering upon people of principle sooner or later weakens popular respect for and support of the government, thus undermining its real authority.

F. Role of the Church Peace Mission

Turning now to the Church Peace Mission, our role as a movement is to persuade the church to withdarw moral support from war. It is not our job to try to ameliorate foreign policy or to persuade a war-making government to include some political or economic element of reconciliation within its war-making program. These elements of reconciliation will follow if the church is true to its calling. As Jesus put it, "Seek ye first the Kingdom of God and all these things shall be added unto you."

Nor is it our job to draw up the blueprint of the new warless society and ask Congress to put this in the form of a resolution. Even if such a resolution were to pass, it would be meaningless unless the groups and pressures that make up society and give real power to government had changed in the direction of the resolution Congress had passed. It is not our job at this stage to draw the conclusion, but to build the major premise on which a peaceful society must rest. The real job is not that of a program like pushing Point 4 or universal disarmament. Public opinion can be for these and for war at the same time. Our program should be that of withdrawing moral as well as personal support from the war system and at the same time building economic, political, social, and racial attitudes consistent with man's worth and human brotherhood. This requires us to function as a radical leaven within the church so that the church may fulfill its function of serving as a revolutionary leaven to society.

In the final analysis only God is relevant. To the degree that the church as a community of redeemed people is a witness in the world to the Kingdom of God, it too will be relevant. The same is true for individuals. The test of relevance is therefore not political power. Rather, if a person or group is relevant in terms of God, its influence or power will not be lost upon the wider community. Thus, the criterion for action is not whether a certain course or program is likely to gain or wield political power in the Niebuhrian sense, but whether it is right in the sight of God for the individual person and society.

At this point of what is right, all of us must exercise the greatest humility in judging our own as well as the action of others. We can and must be constantly open to the will of God through prayer, the critical judgment of others, and to the consequences or probable consequences our action will have on other persons.

XIII

The Kansas City Riot Could Have Been Averted

(Focus Midwest, Volume 6, Number 42, 1968)

The April riots in Kansas City were by no means the largest or most serious in the nation, yet they dramatized a problem inherent in other riots, that of bad relations between the police and residents of the black ghetto.

When the April riots in Kansas City were over, six black persons were dead, scores wounded, and $915,000 worth of property had been destroyed. One of the most serious consequences was the damage to community relations. Moderate Negroes and community leaders, who had been vocal supporters of the police, discovered during the riots that all black men were treated alike. Some believed that the police, 94.5% a white force, were in fact making war on the entire black community. According to the *Kansas City Star,* Herman Johnson, metropolitan NAACP president said, "the apparent aim of the police department during recent rioting was to ring the entire Negro area to prevent damage in the white community and to patrol the area to prevent damage to businesses." Johnson also said, "police should have ringed trouble areas within the Negro district and given the same protection to peaceful Negro neighborhoods as was given white neighborhoods." Instead, he asserted, "because of police, it was extremely dangerous to be a Negro anywhere in the Negro community during the rioting, despite the fact that only a tiny group actually caused the trouble."

The police, on the other hand, viewed their action as a major triumph in law enforcement. The Kansas City police claimed theirs was the first city in the nation where not one block or building was abandoned by law enforcement officers. "We never gave up a block," said C. M. Kelley, Chief of Police. Although many white clergymen were critical of the police for precipitate use of tear gas, the white community in general stood with the police or remained silent.

The Events of April 9

At approximately 8:00 on the morning of Tuesday, April 9, students from Lincoln High School, an all-Negro institution, began to march to other black schools, apparently to express their feelings after the murder of Martin Luther King. They were unhappy over the decision the day before to keep the schools open. That decision had been made by white Board of Education personnel in consultation with the Chief of Police, who believed there would be less trouble if students were kept off the streets.

When students, apparently from Central High (another Negro school), rushed through the hallways of Central Junior High about 8:30 a.m. shouting "school's out," the school principal phoned the police, fearful that the crowd would tear up the building. No damage was done, and the group was quickly herded out of the building. A second group of older youths invaded the Junior High School about 25 minutes later. Some of them grabbed books and threw them out of windows. At about 9:15 a.m., the principal of Central High dismissed school, urging students to go home to watch the King funeral on television.

The students from two other high schools, Lincoln and Manual, came in sight, and those from Central joined the march. At this point, some students and older community leaders suggested that a memorial service be held at Central instead of continuing the march. The marchers paused and headed toward Central. According to the *Kansas City Star*, police car No. 77, with four officers, approached the crowd. Chemical Mace was sprayed on the crowd from the car. "Initially," said the *Star*, "the students had one cause, which they voiced loudly: they wanted the day off to mark the funeral of Dr. King. But the use of Mace apparently gave them another rallying issue."

As the mood of the crowd changed, there were shouted suggestions to march downtown. Over the objections of some of the older leaders, Vernon Thompson began to lead the march downtown. Shortly after 10:00 a.m., while the march was in process, Missouri Highway Patrolmen moved into the downtown area and Governor Warren E. Hearnes activated the National Guard. A few minutes later, a detective arrested Vernon Thompson.

As the march progressed, police made a line across the street at Thirty-first near Troost and fired tear gas. The crowd dispersed in many directions, but the main body, which had stopped a few blocks away, listened to speeches urging order and calm before resuming the march. It was described by the April 9 *Star* as "a largely peaceful march of more than 1,000 Negroes."

Mayor Ilus Davis, who had been informed the students wanted to meet with him at Parade Park, went there to speak to the crowd. With

86

his back to a police car and then from the hood of the car, he tried to talk to the group. One of the young leaders, Leo Bohannon, known as Lebo, came to believe the Mayor and the police with their gas masks, were simply trying to contain them. Lebo asked why the march could not continue downtown. "Is it because, Mr. Mayor, you want to keep the black problems in the black part of town? Are you ashamed of us, Mr. Mayor? Is that why you keep us out here with your policemen and the clubs and the gas? We want to find out. We want to go downtown!" Within a minute or two, the Mayor was helped off the car and, arm in arm with two men, began to march again.

A few blocks away, there was another line of police wearing gas masks. The police, who were under strict orders not to let anyone pass, refused to let the Mayor through the line until a high-ranking police officer intervened. In Kansas City, the Mayor has no authority over the police. It is one of two cities in the United States where the Governor controls the police department.

After the crowd got past the police, about 700 persons broke and ran, leaving the Mayor and others behind. The Mayor proceeded to City Hall via police car and walked east to meet the crowd, who were approaching City Hall. By this time, according to a police report, 100 to 150 "colored males and females" were attempting to force their way into Jones Department Store. They were dispersed with tear gas.

In the meantime, Mayor Davis was speaking to about 300 to 400 marchers near City Hall. A disc jockey for KPRS, a Negro-owned radio station, suggested that everyone go to the Holy Name Roman Catholic Church for a rock 'n roll dance.

The Canisters Began to Fly

Before the students could get to the church, a police line of 80 to 90 men wearing gas masks massed nearby. The *Kansas City Star* description said, "A photograph taken moments before the policemen began to use gas reveals that about 100 Negroes were on the sidewalk, the lawn, or in the street on the west half of the block, closest to the police line. It also shows only a few of them near the policemen." Nevertheless, the tear gas canisters began to fly.

The police explanations afterwards are confused. Some officers said tear gas was thrown because a pop bottle was thrown in the direction of the police. Episcopal Bishop Robert Spears saw the pop bottle break near an officer's feet. Another officer claimed that he saw two Negroes steal two gas canisters that had been laid down by another officer and that he later saw these youths throw the canisters into their own crowd. Few Negroes believe this story or can understand how two Negroes could get close enough to the police to steal tear gas without being apprehended.

An officer who used Mace said he had been subjected to taunts and obscenities, and one Negro had spat on him. Another officer said the gas was provoked by a Negro woman who walked close to the police "cursing them and striking at them but not quite hitting them." Some critics wonder why the police could not tolerate abusive words that resulted in no injuries. Others ask why individual offenders were not arrested, instead of tear-gassing an entire crowd.

After the tear gas was thrown and the crowd began to run away from it, the police began to use clubs on the crowd. Two Episcopal priests in clerical garb, Canon David Fly, the white pastor of the Cathedral, and the Rev. Edward L. Warner, the Negro paster of St. Augustine's Church, were clubbed. One patrolman afterwards said, "Due to the confusion and the impaired vision caused by the gas mask, I did not know he was a priest." Father Warner asserted that he was struck again after he had fallen. Canon Fly was clubbed when he went to Father Warner's aid after he saw a patrolman hit Warner. After Canon Fly had been struck to the ground and was blinded by tear gas, he said, "Five of my black friends came to my aid and picked me up and said, 'Let's give our brother a hand,' and carried me away." At the hospital, where he was taken by a TV reporter, Canon Fly was found to have cracked cartilages in the right rib cage.

A white Roman Catholic priest, Lawrence McNamara, who was present at City Hall, stated that if instructions to police at City Hall had been to treat students as "by and large a good group of kids, the police could not only have contained them but changed some deep-seated feelings."

About an hour after the City Hall incident, Father McNamara, who had gone to Holy Name Church, said he saw many police cars descending on the church. He ran outside and into tear gas to try to contact officers to tell them there was no problem. When the gas cleared away, he said, "I was never so scared in my life. I observed the officers throwing the bolt forward on their rifles and all advancing toward us."

"I shouted to the police, 'Don't shoot'. " the police did not shoot, but Father Timothy Gibbons, associate pastor of the church, reported (according to the diocesan paper, *The New People*) that during the dance "several canisters of gas were tossed into the hall from windows on the west side and that police broke windows on the south side, also, and lobbed in containers." Father Gibbons said he asked a policeman with a gas mask for assistance in getting the students out but received none. "It was impossible to see," said Father Gibbons. "Everyone was blind, choking. Kids crowded up under the bandstand. Some hid in the closet. It was a terrible job getting them out." The priest asked who had authorized the use of gas in such quantities in the church. He said, "One officer told me that they had all the authorization they needed."

The police position is that a police car passing near the church was pelted by bricks. Other cars responded to their call, with officers firing gas to disperse small groups of young people who were watching the incident. The police claimed that they had no knowledge of the dance. Sgt. England, according to the *Kansas City Star*, said, "the police did not know if the people in the church 'were armed or destroying property'. "

The Mood Changed

After these various tear gas incidents, the temper of many black people changed to open hostility toward the police. As the *Kansas City Star* round-up stated, "Events Tuesday afternoon built swiftly toward a riot situation."

On Wednesday, April 10, police tear-gassed students at Lincoln High School. Police reports are in conflict over the cause of the gassing. One officer claims that a patrolman was injured by a stone before the gas was used. But the police log records gas being used before Patrolman Fordyce, who was injured by a stone, was on the scene. The unanswered question: Was another patrolman also injured? But in any event, six girls, who were burned and gassed by a grenade thrown by the police into a girls' restroom in the school, were taken to the hospital. All policemen who were questioned, however, denied throwing a tear gas missile into the school. Harry I. Harwell, the school principal, called the use of gas a ". . . wanton attack on my children. If it had been a white school, they wouldn't have done it."

That night four Negro men were shot and three white men wounded. The incident began when two patrolmen and two national guardsmen advanced with fixed bayonets into a parking lot across the street from the Byron Hotel in the black ghetto. One of the guardsmen, William F. Jewett, was shot in the right forearm and fell to the ground. Jewett said that at the time he thought the shots came from the Byron Hotel, but indicated that later he was uncertain about their origin.

The manager of the hotel, Emmett Finney, who had just finished boarding up some windows in front of the hotel, noted people still milling around in the area near the hotel which the police had just roped off. Apparently the police decided to clear the area by using tear gas. Finney and others ran into the hotel and started up the stairs to the lobby, which was well back on the second floor. Finney said he heard someone shout that a guardsman had been shot, adding that if a shot had come from the hotel he would have heard it. He had not, however, heard the shot. The police headed toward the hotel and fired tear gas into the small front entrance, trapping a number of people who had sought refuge from the gas in the street. A 50-year-old Negro minister and his 16-year-old son, George McKinney, Jr., were shot and killed, Finney believes, when they ran from the hotel entrance to escape the gas. The police say that those running from the hotel were caught in the cross-fire between snipers and the police, whereas Finney asserts that it was physically impossible for anyone running from the hotel to be caught in any except police crossfire. The hotel building was surrounded by police, who ordered everyone in the back to lie down in the parking lot. Finney said he offered to open all doors in the hotel with his keys, but the officers instead chose to break in all the doors. The only fire-arms found were in the hotel office, and none had been fired. No snipers were found in the hotel, although the police steadfastly maintain they saw muzzle flashes in the windows of the hotel.

The third death in the area was 43-year-old Charles Shugg Martin, who had been drinking all day and did not respond immediately when ordered to move.

The fourth death occurred when 38-year-old Julius Hamilton, appar-ently in response to an order to come out, opened the door of a first floor apartment. Actually, the police were telling an officer who was between the building to come out "and we will cover you." Hamilton was killed by a slug from a police riot gun, although he had no gun and there was no evidence he was threatening anyone.

None of the four men killed was carrying a weapon.

Rep. Harold Holliday, a Negro member of the Missouri legislature, said that "what happened at the Byron Hotel would not have occurred at the Plaza. The police just opened fire on anyone who happened to be in the way."

During the riots, a group of Kansas City clergymen and theological students manned a communications center at the Metropolitan Inter-Church Agency. They also had observers in strategic locations through-out the city and at the police stations, magistrate's court, City Hall, and three hospitals. When the city and county jails were filled and unable to handle curfew violators, the police agreed to release them into the custody of the clergy. The violators could not be taken into the riot areas, so receiving centers were set up in available churches downtown, where they could spend the night. Clergymen, lawyers, and social workers were on duty all night at these centers.

Clergymen were told by persons who were brought to the centers that pocket knives, watches, and other personal items were taken from them without being receipted. One man reported being made to lie on the street while police kicked him and shot in the dirt beside him. His girl friend was forced to "take her drawers off" so she could be frisked. She was taken with four patrolmen in a patrol car while he went in a paddy wagon. He did not see her again before he was taken to one of the church centers, and she was not sent there. A high school boy reported seeing police force a girl to remove some of her clothes. A young man with a piece of glass in his eye was brought to Grace and Holy Trinity for curfew violation, but the police did not take him to the hospital.

"Dehumanizing and Discriminatory"

On the second day of the riots, the Metropolitan Inter-Church Agency's administrative committee, at a special session, charged the Kansas City police department with "dehumanizing and discriminatory practices" toward Negroes during and after the demonstrations by students.

Although there were many allegations of police brutality against Negroes, only one was witnessed by a white man willing to appear on behalf of the beaten black man. Lester Blue, a 35-year-old employee at Wendell Phillips Elementary School, stopped at a traffic light at the same time as a police patrol car. Blue stated that Patrolman Richard Goering jumped from his car with his riot gun in hand, saying, "Get out, you black — !" The victim said the officer stuck his riot gun in the window of the car and placed it against his cheek. After Blue got out of his car, the officer allegedly began hitting him in the face and back with his gun butt. Blue also stated that Goering cocked his riot gun and pulled the trigger, but it clicked and did not go off. Goering then drove off without making an arrest, according to both Blue and the witness. As a result of the protest by Sidney Willens, a white attorney, the patrolman was suspended pending an investigation.

It was not simply the absence of witnesses that made it difficult to sustain charges of police brutality. A number of black persons report that police had taken off their badges. Father Lawrence McNamara, a white priest, confirmed this. During the Holy Name Church incident, he said, "Two sergeants I got close to did not have name tags."

Another tragedy of the riots was the handling of those arrested by the police. The Kansas City Star reported on April 11 that "No attempts have been made to release any of the committed persons on bail. Since attorneys have not been appointed, motions have not been filed to reduce bonds to a figure that the defendants might meet." The week following the riots, 160 persons were still in the Jackson County Jail because of excessive bail, ranging from $50,000 to $100,000. Preliminary hearings had not even been held because police officers were kept on stand-by basis and, therefore, were unable to make court appearances. The following are examples of the bail set for specific charges: possession of a fire bomb, $100,000; carrying a concealed weapon, $50,000; stealing more than $50, $50,000; stealing under $50, $5,000.

There were cases of wrong arrest. One case involved about 10 youths who, while fleeing police bullets, ran onto the porch of a house. The owner, who feared they would damage his property, stepped out onto the porch in time to be arrested with the youths. He was in custody two days before his story could be heard.

As late as May 10, the *Kansas City Call* reported that the mother and the widow of two of the men killed by policemen on April 10 claimed they had not been officially notified of the deaths or the circumstances surrounding them.

"I Am Sorry"

Reactions to the incidents of the riot week were mixed. Mayor Davis, on a TV program, referred to the use of gas at City Hall and said, "I am sorry that there was any tear gas, and actually I would say 95% to 98% of the students were very orderly and were very restrained."

Chief of Police C. M. Kelley stated, "No operation of the magnitude of the riot control could be completed without some errors. I believe them, however, to be minimized and of the type that occur when men have little time to engage in careful reflection . . ."

The director of the Methodist Metropolitan Planning Commission and senior National Guard chaplain in Missouri, the Rev. Shrum Burton, said he "understood the intensity of feeling of the black community, who felt the overemphasis of tear gas and dispersing of student demonstrations offended their own sense of dignity and worth . . . It is strange that our society says it cannot afford programs that are creative in the ghetto but can afford to call National Guard troops to duty at the cost of more than $90,000 per day."

A group of leaders of Negro organizations and whites active in civil rights movements sent a long telegram to the U.S. Department of Justice asking a full investigation of the police action and expressing concern about the praise of the police by the Governor of Missouri "after having knowledge of the complaints of the chairmen of various civic and civil rights organizations."

Elijah Parnell, a Negro in his 70's, expressed the mood of many in the black ghetto when he said, "The police have used a reign of terror on Negroes for a long time, and it is just natural for them to do what they did because they have been taught that. Negroes are only paying back some of the things whites have done to them."

The most charitable comments about the police coming from their critics are that they were underpaid, poorly educated, often from rural Missouri or other communities with stereotypes about Negroes, and inadequately trained to deal with black people as human beings.

A high-ranking police official was quoted in the *Kansas City Star* of May 5 as saying, "The police department hasn't been given enough money to get the mature, educated men whose judgment can stand retrospective review."

The chief of police, who was subject to a great deal of criticism, was apparently torn between maintaining the morale of his men and placating his critics. The *Kansas City Star* said, "Whatever the chief's personal opinions about the conduct of his men, he appeared to feel his primary duty was to maintain order. To have hurt the morale of his men could have reduced their effectiveness in this role."

Much of the criticism leveled at Chief Kelley should have been directed at the Assistant Chief of Police, Lt. Col. James Newman, who made trips to other riot-torn areas to decide on Kansas City procedure. Newman made speeches prior to the riots reflecting the attitudes of riot control and community relations that were demonstrated in the handling of the crowds before the shooting began.

The over-all picture of $915,000 damage during the riots reveal $829,000 to building, inventories, motor cars, and in looting. Of that, $530,000 was caused by 98 arson fires, $79,000 by looting and damage to liquor stores, about $53,000 in broken glass, and $163,000 inventory loss due to fire.

In six days of civil disorder in Kansas City, there were 287 felony arrests, or an average of fewer than 50 a day. The 1966 FBI report shows 18,385 felony (plus 9,267 larceny thefts under $50) arrests in Kansas City, or an average of 50 a day in a non-riot year.

All of the civilians wounded by gunfire were Negro, as were all those who were killed. Two National Guardsmen and one fireman were wounded by sniper fire, but no police officer was the victim of gunfire. One young Negro woman, Miss LaNita Jackson, a research assistant for the Institute for Community Studies, said, "You can see that only property was destroyed. They weren't trying to kill whites, because if they were, they could have."

Police Captain Norman Caron estimated that snipers actually fired at 25 to 30 locations but said that there may have been only from 5 to 20 actual snipers. The maximum law enforcement level to cope with snipers, looters, arsonists, and thwarted high school students was 940 city policemen, 180 Missouri Highway patrolmen, 30 Jackson County sheriff's deputies, and nearly 3,000 National Guardsmen.

No Riot in Kansas

In contrast to events in Kansas City, Missouri, there was no rioting in Kansas City, Kansas, which also has a large black population. In Kansas City, Kansas, there was the same student unrest after the assassination of Dr. King, but the school authorities dismissed school, and the police, instead of trying to suppress the student marches, assisted the students.

After a school assembly on Friday, April 5, in memory of Dr. King, about 1,000 Negro students from Sumner and Wyandotte High Schools marched through the downtown area. The parade was led by two uniformed officers, one white and one Negro, both on motorcycles. Other Negro officers in plain clothes were also in the march.

Major Boston Daniels, a Negro officer who came to Wyandotte High School, told the students, "We are most happy to be here. We did not come here to disturb your march. We came to march with you." Daniels asked that students be selected to lead the march. From Wyandotte, the march moved to Sumner High School and thence to City Hall, where Mayor Joseph McDowell told the students he was happy they were there to express what was in their hearts "and what is in the hearts of all Americans." After the meeting at City Hall, Major Daniels said, "We appreciate the way you have conducted yourselves. I hope you'll return to your classes now. That's where we're going to win." Then Major Daniels started walking with the students.

The April 5 *Kansas City Star* description said, "Daniels remained cool and kindly over the bullhorn, putting some of his remarks on a personal basis, with effectiveness. 'Will you do me a favor and stay in the street,' he said when some of the youths strayed onto the sidewalk along Minnesota."

The attitude of the black people of Kansas City, Kansas, toward the police department improved, rather than deteriorated. This began earlier when police guilty of continual police brutality were dismissed. But the most striking difference in the two cities was the attitude toward the students and toward Dr. King's death. By encouraging and supporting a responsible expression of the feelings of the students, the police demonstrated their own concern and sorrow over the death of Dr. King.

Another contrast between the cities shows 53 Negro police officers out of 940 in Kansas City, Missouri, but 46 Negro officers in a force of 208 in Kansas City, Kansas.

The Kansas City, Missouri, police indicate that they want to recruit more Negro officers, but the police image in the black ghetto is not such as to be very enticing.

The Kansas City, Missouri, riot story is a sad one, not because the police are worse than the white community at large, or because of black militants. These are myths. The police represent the racial attitudes of the governor, most of the white citizens of Kansas City, and the suburban business elite that rule the city. Significantly, in Kansas City, Kansas, it was black militants who helped to preserve order!

The sad part about the police in Kansas City, Missouri is that they sent top officers to other riot-torn cities to learn how to deal with riots, but apparently they learned nothing from the report of the National Advisory Commission on Civil Disorders about preventing the kind of police practices that precipitate riots.

XIV

Christian Responsibility with Respect to Marxism

(Chapter from *The Theology of Mission: The Christian and Political Responsibility*, Division of World Missions, Board of Mission, The Methodist Church, June 1962)

Introduction

It is extremely difficult for an American Christian to speak or write about Marxism. He lives in a land which has for almost twenty years identified the leading Marxist state as its major enemy. He is a product of Western and democratic thought, has grown accustomed to a specific parliamentary and juridical system, and has been conditioned by the most capitalist of existing economic systems. All of these, for example, are alien to the Russian and Chinese Marxist ways of life.

Even if an American Christian seeks consciously to avoid identifying Christianity with his own culture, there are subtle relationships which nevertheless influence his thinking. He must therefore continually remind himself that Christianity existed for about 1600 years before Western democracy began, for about 1800 years before the United States was formed, that it is alive in the Soviet Union and other Marxist lands without the aid of American churches, that Christianity flourished for centuries before there was any such thing as capitalism, and that it lives today in agrarian, "communist," democratic socialist, capitalist and mixed economies.

When Christians discuss Marxism they confront something more than a philosophy whose explanation of the world differs from that of the Christian faith. Whittaker Chambers defined "the revolutionary heart of Communism" as "a simple statement of Karl Marx further simplified for handy use: 'philosophers have explained the world; it is necessary to change the world.'"[1]

This is another way of saying that Marxism is not simply a theory or system of thought but is also an approach to social change. Because it combines an interpretation of history with an impulse to aid the

[1] *The Witness*, p. 9.

processes of history, it has much of the dogma and driving force of a religion.

Yet it is not a religion, since it denies all standards of judgment outside or beyond the process of history and therefore has no final authority other than the Party by which to determine morality, estimate the value of persons, maintain checks on power, or provide a continuing higher destiny for man. Although it is not a religion in any true sense, it makes totalitarian claims upon its adherents, imposes an orthodoxy of belief, and practice, and even uses a ritualistic language.

Properly speaking, Marxism is an ideology which we may define as the creative application of a theory of reality to the problems of society. Marxism then is not simply the doctrines of Karl Marx; it is these doctrines as extended and modified by Lenin, Stalin, and Krushchev in the course of their encounter with the developments of history. Paradoxically, Marxism is both dogmatic and flexible. Khrushchev, for example, can take the dogma of Lenin and Stalin that war is inevitable in a world of capitalist states and assert in the light of nuclear war and the growth of Communist power that war is no longer inevitable. On this issue Soviet Marxists differ with their Chinese counterparts because national perspectives, including economic, political and military problems are very different. It is this flexibility which has led some analysts to minimize the Marxism and maximize Soviet or Chinese nationalism as the basis for interpreting the policies of these states. Nevertheless the basic Marxist assumptions of economic determinism, historical materialism, the class struggle, and dialectical materialism remain and play an important role in domestic and foreign policy in all Marxist states.

Although Marxism is grounded in certain assumptions that are alien to the Christian faith, such as the idea that political, cultural, religious and other developments of society are determined by economic or material factors, there has been no uniform Christian response to it. Christians differ not only in their philosophical analysis of Marxism but in their views as to its practical program.

Christian Views of Marxism

In general there are three approaches that Christians have taken with respect to Marxism. These approaches in turn have largely determined the kind of action taken with respect to it.

I. The first of these approaches is that Communism is a kind of irresistible wave of the future. This is true not only of a few Christians in the West like the Red Dean of Canterbury in England who think of Communism as man's best political hope, but is also true of others who have consciously rejected Marxism. When Whittaker Chambers broke with the Communist Party in 1937 after having entered it in 1925, he looked about him at the world in which we live and saw that neither the West nor Christianity was solving the problems that had given rise to Communism — the problems of poverty, nationalism, imperialism, and war. "You know," he said to his wife, "we are leaving the winning world for the losing world." He added later, "Almost nothing that I have observed or that has happened to me since has made me think that I was wrong about that forecast."

Other Americans, far less astute than Whittaker Chambers, have become captives of their fears and frustrations. Every mistake of the West or its leaders, they believe, is a result of superior Communist organization or intrigue. These right-wing extremists show filmstrips such as COMMUNISM ON THE MAP, which assert that one country after another throughout the world has gone Communist and the United States is the next target.

Still others around the world believe that however bad Communism is it will in time improve, and in any event it is bound to be victorious.

Whether these judgments are based upon fears that Khrushchev may be right in his assertion that "We will bury you," or whether they are based on hope of a classless society of peace and plenty, they are a factor with which we must reckon in the Christian world. Two things at least need to be said of this general approach that Marxism is the wave of the future:

A) The first is that in some degree the whole socialist impulse which has been so largely set in motion by Marxists is having a very great appeal to many people in the underdeveloped areas of the world. One reason for the appeal of socialism is the knowledge that no underdeveloped nation and very few industrial nations have enough private capital to make the capitalist system or an approximation of it possible except on the basis of American investments and control. In Africa only the Union of South Africa has this capitalist hope. In Asia only Japan has capitalist possibilities and then only if supported by the United States. In Europe, Switzerland, Holland and West Germany are the most likely holdouts for capitalism. In the Western hemisphere there are Canada and the United States. Premier Khrushchev notes this world economic trend as evidence that Marxist economic laws are at work and confidently says to Western capitalism, "We will bury you."

Those Christians who believe that the decline of world capitalism necessarily or inevitably contributes to the advance of Marxism evidently make the mistake of assuming that capitalism, Western democracy and even Christian values are inseparably related. In so doing they have tended to accept the Marxist analysis that the political, cultural and religious institutions of society are the product of economic developments. But in a deeper sense they have tended to deify or make ultimate a particular economic order of society. These Christians who see no democratic socialist alternative to capitalism, no neutralist possibility in the American-Russian power struggle, no hope for Christianity except in the context of Western democracy, tend to abandon to Marxism such nations as Cuba, and to be very skeptical about India or Burma.

Those who assert that all is lost if capitalism is lost and those who assert that the goal of history toward which economic forces have been driving us is a classless society need equally to be reminded that no human society is final. Every human society measured against the will of God has been and will be proven inadequate. In Tennyson's words, "Our little systems have their day, they have their day and cease to be, for Thou, O Lord, art more than they!"

B) A second thing we can say about this concept that Marxism is the wave of the future, is a paraphrase of Isaiah 31:3: "The Marxists are men and not gods, and their horses are flesh and not spirit." This is evident in the mistakes that Communists have made, the revolts they have faced, and the defeats they have suffered. The Polish revolt against Soviet control was so strong that Gomulka refused to let Khrushchev address the Central Committee of the Polish Party in spite of Khrushchev's presence in Warsaw, his insistent demands to meet with the Central Committee, and the fact that Russian troops had encircled Warsaw and were marching upon it. Flora Lewis in her *Case History of Hope* details the dramatic story of Khrushchev's defeat by a united Poland. If we have learned anything from the Polish revolution, from the revolt against Stalinism inside the Soviet Union, from the Yugoslav refusal to obey Russian orders, from the differences that exist between China and Russia, it is this — that Marxism is not one mighty force to be reckoned with but is a movement of rival factions within which social change is possible and against which revolt has been successful.

II. A second approach that Christians have taken with respect to Marxism is that it is so diabolical that it must at all points be opposed. This is an easy judgment to make because there is a great deal in Marxism that is evil. Atheism, totalitarianism, the idea that the end justifies any means, the greater significance placed upon the class than upon the individual, are illustrations of the evil that makes Communism seem so satanic to many Christians.

When President Eisenhower invited Premier Khrushchev to the United States in 1959, Cardinal Spellman asserted that the day Khrushchev landed on our soil would be a day no less infamous than that barbaric day of betrayal at Pearl Harbor. He called upon all the faithful to attend prayer meetings the night before the Premier's visit. At the prayer meeting in St. Patrick's Cathedral, Father Gannon, former President of Fordham, likened the conflict between the United States and the Soviet Union to the conflict between heaven and hell. Archbishop Boland of Newark called upon parochial school children in his archdiocese to say three Hail Marys every school day that Khrushchev remained in the United States.

In similar fashion, some Protestant laymen, ministers, and bishops have been outspoken in trying to exclude "Red" China from the United Nations or in preventing recognition of China or trade with her.

The conviction that Marxism is diabolical has both religious and political overtones. In practice, Marxist leaders and in some cases whole populations living under Marxist rule are viewed as devils. The cold war is then not simply rivalry between two hostile political systems or power blocs but assumes the proportions of a holy war. Governments are no longer recognized on the century-old basis that they are effectively holding the reins of power. Instead, recognition and even trade are determined on the basis of a false moralism that equates enmity with the diabolical.

The implication of this approach is that the Communists are the "bad guys" and we are the "good guys"; that they are lined up with the devil and we are on the side of the angels.

A) This is bad politics not only because it assumes nations are to be accepted or ostracized on the basis of the subjective moral standards of their opponents but also because it implies that we must not enter negotiations with the devil. God and his angels do not negotiate with the devil. The devil exists only to be fought and conquered. Yet if we are to have peace in our nuclear world we shall have to negotiate with Communists.

B) It is also bad theology to assume that the evil in Marxism permits a division of the world into a devil bloc and a righteous bloc. "All have sinned and fallen short of the glory of God." Evil in our world did not come into existence with Karl Marx or the Communist Party. Nor are the Communists the only ones to blame for the world's ills. We bear our share. There are Christians in the John Birch Society and the Christian Crusades of Billy James Hargis and Dr. Fred Schwarz who believe that the United States is confronted with serious world problems because of a Communist conspiracy in high places rather than any fault of our own. No Christian who takes seriously the fact that sin is universal can blame the world's problems on some other group. Nor can any Christian who takes seriously the commandment to love one's neighbor as oneself permit the evil doctrines or acts of others to exclude them from international contacts or community or justify the trade restrictions which intensify the starvation of millions of their people.

C) A refusal to view the conflict between the Marxist world and the Western world in terms of irreconcilable warfare or in terms of a moral struggle between the forces of evil and the forces of good does not of course mean that there are no moral differences either in doctrine or in practice. Rather it means that the moral differences in doctrine must not be used by Christians to justify: 1) immoral practice by political units under the cloak of doctrinal morality, or 2) the hate and bitterness necessary for a continuing cold war, or 3) the treating of whole peoples as if they are necessarily and irrevocably infected by demonic faith. These people, including their Marxist leaders, cannot be totally rejected as Communists if we remember that they are also creatures of God for whom Christ died. We must not, in other words, permit opposition to Communist doctrine to keep us, as Charles West has observed in his book, *Communism and the Theologians*, from "that depth of understanding and service to the real person behind the Communist, which is the fruit of Christian love" (p. 48).

III. A third approach that Christians have taken is that Marxism is the judgment of God upon a Christian church which has failed to take seriously its responsibility to be salt and leaven to a society in need of transformation. It can also be said that Communism is the judgment of God upon a Western civilization that refused to take seriously that measure of insight gleaned from the best of its Greek, Roman and Hebrew heritage to which we refer in such phrases as the French "liberty, equality, fraternity," or the American right to "life, liberty, and the pursuit of happiness."

A) Both church and government in England, Holland, Belgium, France, Italy, Portugal, Spain and the United States had a chance during the century or two before the Communist Party came to power to treat other human beings as our brothers. Instead we subjected them in colonies, or treated them as economic vassals destined to live in poverty, or enslaved Africans and brought them to this country to work. In more recent years we have had one opportunity after another to end war through disarmament and have refused to do so. Now we are caught in the position where, in order to keep colonial peoples from going Communist, we have had to free them. In order to keep our economic vassals in Latin America from going Communist we must press for social change there. And to avoid the kind of destruction by the Soviet Union that we have visited upon Hiroshima and Nagasaki, upon Korea and Germany, we shall have to negotiate with the Russians on the basis of their program for total disarmament.

When we see the hand of God in Communism forcing us to do what we would not voluntarily as Christians have done on the basis of our own deepest convictions, then we know today what the ancient Israelites learned before us, that God has used tyrannical and unjust powers for his glory. In the ninth chapter of Isaiah there are strong words used against fellow countrymen who have refused to follow the will of God:

"Woe to those who call evil good and good evil, who put darkness for light and light for darkness . . . Woe to those who are wise in their own eyes and shrewd in their own sight." Isaiah goes on to describe the oppression of the needy and the robbing of the poor and then adds: "So the Lord raises adversaries against them and stirs up their enemies." At another point Isaiah sees Assyria as the judgment of God to bring Israel to terms: "Oh Assyria (or in our day, Russia) the rod of my anger, the staff of my fury. Against a godless nation I send him and against the people of my wrath I command him. . . ."

Nicholas Berdyaev was the first to perceive in the Marxist criticsim of religion a judgment of God upon the Christian church as well as upon the Russian people. It was the moral condition of the Russians that made Marxist rule both possible and necessary. "God, if I may dare say so, transferred authority to the Bolshevists for the punishment of the people," he writes in his essay on *The Russian Revolution*. "This is why their power possesses a mysterious strength which the Bolshevists themselves cannot understand."

Marxism, however, was not simply a Russian problem. It has had and continues to have a universal appeal. In a very real sense it has become the adversary of Christianity because Christianity has failed to provide the dynamic for the new and better life which people everywhere are demanding. Christians here and there have pointed the way but the church as a whole has not risen to the need.

Both Marxists and Christians are believers in the midst of a skeptical world that nevertheless wants something revolutionary enough to transform the world. The power of the Communist world is the unifying common faith that inspires their social order, whereas in the West there is in fact very little connection between our religious faith and our economic or political order. There is a deep chasm dividing the Christian ethic from the theory and practice of monopoly capitalism and the military-industrial complex that so largely determines Western domestic and foreign policies.

The dynamic missionary enterprise of the Christian church suffers from its attachment to an institution that has made its accommodation to the economic-military-political order of our day. Nowhere is this more clear than the church's willingness to write off its future if not present opportunity in China by allying itself with the temporary cold war policy of the United States in the Far East.

This means that at the very moment when Marxism confronts a disintegrated world with an inadequate but unified faith and program, Christianity offers the world an adequate faith so allied to lesser political and economic loyalties as to appear unable to provide the cement which is needed to reconstruct and hold together a new social order.

B) Some Christians think of Communism as judgment in the sense that it can be modified or transformed to become a more hopeful society. To this end they identify themselves politically and tentatively with Marxist efforts while rejecting the basic Marxist philosophy. Hromadka describes Communism as judgment in these terms:

> Communism is also the dynamic — so difficult to define — of contemporary history; it is that which is in the air; it is that which humanly speaking acts as an irresistible effort to put the disintegrated world not on the basis of personal privileges, interests, profits, and advantage, but on social equality, security, and collective cooperation of the popular multitudes.

It is therefore "partly an heir of the age-long craving for social justice and equality, partly a child of the errors, blindness and greediness of bourgeois society." "Communism reflects in a very secularized form, in spite of its materialism and dictatorship, the Christian longing for the fellowship of full and responsible love." Its thinking is instrumental, its atheism is, in large measure, rather a tool and weapon of an anti-bourgeois or anti-feudal political propaganda than a distinctive faith or metaphysics.[2]

C) Others have viewed Communism as judgment in less romantic terms. They have sought to bridge the chasm between the Christian faith and the economic order of capitalism on the one hand and Communism on the other by providing a third possibility. For a time in the United States, Great Britain, and some other Western nations there were Christian movements that sought to establish a vital connection between the Christian faith and democratic socialism or between Christianity and the cooperative movement. These efforts, so largely a product of the era of theological liberalism, have waned.

D) In their place is the Barthian emphasis of avoiding identification with any new order because any revolutionary act is really a reaction to the existing order and likely to be as unjust or tyrannical as the old. The Christian is to influence the existing order through obedience to Christ. This is no mere formula of words. Instead of supporting the existing order (through ceremonial blessings of the affairs of state such as prayers at state functions and chaplaincies in the armed forces, or through doing other things that create the illusion that the State is Christian), deprive rulers of their power by Christian obedience! The task of the Christian is simply to bear witness to God's revelation in Jesus Christ. Christians whose hope is really in the coming Kingdom of God are not anxious about this or that political order. Because they have no vested interest in things as they are, they are more responsible citizens

---

[2] Assorted quotations from Hromadka, put together by Charles West in *Communism and the Theologian*, pp. 57, 58.

of this world. Because they are basically citizens of The Kingdom, they must demonstrate a superior justice through love.

Barth is not primarily concerned with the East-West conflict either in terms of ideologies or social systems. Insofar as he has commented on the problems Christians face in East Germany or Hungary, he seems to be concerned with the existential meaning of the Communist-Christian encounter. What does the situation mean for them as Christians in relation to the gospel of Christ? When Barth warns East German Christians not to be drawn to the fleshpots of the West but to view Communism as a "useful scourge," he is saying that even in Marxist lands the whole trend of events is in God's hands. In the Marxist state one can bear witness to God's eternal truths.

The Judgment of God is evident in the fact of political change. "When one political system, the work of men's hands, collapses to make way for another, it means at least that the work of divine patience and wisdom is not yet completed. Once again a limit has been set to some abuse of law and freedom, of community and power. A new political system means that men have been allowed a new chance to order their common life differently and possibly better." . . .[3]

E) We must think of Communism as a challenge rather than as an enemy. In his book *Communism and the Theologian*, Charles West describes Reinhold Niebuhr's position on Communism. "The object of his social-ethical concern," writes West, "has changed from the problems of working men seeking social change to the preservation of the genius of a democratic tradition . . ."; he adds that Niebuhr views Communism "as a religious Utopian threat with which no real encounter is possible. . . ." In short, "It has been accepted as an enemy, not as a challenge."

Niebuhr's position is in effect an American cold-war position, whereas our position as Christians ought to be one of viewing Communism as judgment and therefore as challenge. As West indicates, "Niebuhr's writing in recent years implies that America has achieved a relative solution of the problem of justice in her domestic life." This has "turned his radicalism into a conservatism which cannot understand deeply enough the extent to which the modern world has lost its sense even of a residual *justitia orginalis*[4] . . . Niebuhr appears, in short, something like Hromadka in reverse, in most of his recent political thought."[5]

West is in effect saying that the theologian like Hromadka who serves as an apologist for the Communist world and the theologian like Niebuhr who serves as an apologist for the Western world are too involved

---

[3] *Against the Stream*, p. 84.
[4] West, *Communism and the Theologian*, p. 167.
[5] Idem, p. 169.

in their own culture to view the Communist-capitalist struggle from a clearly transcendent perspective.

Yet it is from this perspective alone that we may see the revolutionary ferment of our times not as something to be turned to the advantage of either camp but as a revolution having objective validity. The Congolese, the Cuban, the Laotian must not be used as a tool in the strategy of the Party or the Pentagon but as a person who is the object of Christian concern.

Suggested Christian Courses of Action

If we view Marxism neither as the irresistible wave of the future to which at least qualified and critical support must be given nor as a diabolical system which must be totally opposed but as an inevitable consequence of our failure to meet human need on the basis of our religious commitment, we must still ask what is our present responsibility. As Christians facing squarely both the problem of our own privileged Western position and the problem of totalitarian Communism, we need to ask what we must do to change ourselves and what we can do to help change the Communist world.

I. The Christian's first responsibility with respect to Marxism is to deepen one's own commitment to God and seek to be an obedient disciple. This means that our primary concern will be that of witness to love rather than defense of any existing political order or fear of any rival system. In the final analysis, only a stronger faith and a clearer witness can displace or modify Marxism as the force which transforms and unifies the world. If in the wisdom of God Marxism is to continue as a major factor in world history for an indefinite period, a strong and devoted church can provide an alternative center of meaning and power.

II. A second responsibility is to help the Church change its own position and practice. To some degree the hope that the Church in the Communist as well as the underdeveloped world may be a vital indigenous force rather than an alien and suspect adjunct of a bourgeois culture is dependent upon the American church actually being a revolutionary force for peace, equality, freedom, and justice.

The Church must cease to be Constantinian in its approach to power. Instead of identifying with the bourgeois power elite of our society and seeking to Christianize society from the top through power, we must develop a form of community in which the Gospel is a real alternative both to the special privilege of capitalism and the totalitarian conformity of the Communist reaction to capitalism. Charles West states it this way:

> ". . . the Church has become alienated first from the real community forms of the proletariat, no less the post-Communist proletariat of a Communist land than the Marxist or labor union proletariat of the

past and present; and second from the chastened and realistic bour-
geoisie itself in its search for answers to the relative and immediate
problems of its order and survival. It has become on the whole a community which has appropriated for itself a part of the world, a "religious" sphere of experiences and practices, or sometimes, in the effort
to be open to the world, a part of the sphere of people's leisure time
activities in general.

In the very deepest sense Marxism is a judgment on the church and
on the poverty of Christian life. It is out of a study of the contemporary
Communist challenge that we in the West may learn what so many of
our brethren in other lands have learned at first hand. Dietrich Bon-
hoeffer, though writing out of a different struggle, has nevertheless sum-
marized what the church must face in respect to Communism:

> During these years the Church has fought for self-preservation as
> though it were an end in itself and has thereby lost its chance to speak
> a word of reconciliation to mankind and the world at large. So our
> traditional language must perforce become powerless and remain silent,
> and our Christianity today will be confined to praying for and doing
> right by our fellow men. Christian thinking, speaking, and organiza-
> tion must be reborn out of this praying and this action.

American Christians have a special responsibility to end what seems
to many around the world to be an alliance with our military, political
and economic system. Missionaries or travelling Christians who serve
the Central Intelligence Agency, ministers and laymen who are apolo-
gists for special interests or the *status quo,* church pronouncements
which call for American military strength to contain Communism, are
illustrations of the problem Christians have to overcome if they are to
make a witness for Christ among people who have no sympathy for
capitalism or militarism or American nationalism.

A favorite illustration of Communists who see the Church as an ally
of Western state power is the military chaplaincy. When ministers receive
their pay, rank, uniform and orders from the military instead of from
the Church, there is inevitable confusion as to the role of the Church,
not only in the minds of overseas people where American troops serve,
but among the soldiers themselves. The Methodist Church might well
revive and adopt Ernest Fremont Tittle's recommendation of a civilian
church chaplaincy or ministry to men in the armed forces.

One ex-Communist, now a Christian, has written:

> We of the West are in one sense fortunate to be spared the vicissitudes
> of life under Communist tyranny. But let us not congratulate ourselves
> too quickly. If we may justifiably commiserate with our brethren in
> the East for their loss of freedom, may we not also ponder the worth
> of some of the questionable prerogatives which they lost as well? They

105

have been kicked out of the affairs of state; there are no chaplains in the East German armed forces or in the one-party legislature, and the Communist leaders do not crib passages from scripture with which to sugarcoat their policies. To some Americans, it would be a relief not to see the Prince of Peace perennially miscast as a standard bearer for our programs of massive armaments; and we might count our East German brothers as the recipients of a profound blessing in this regard.

III. A third responsibility is to affirm both in faith and practice the dignity or sacredness of all human personality. Every person, regardless of political or religious conviction, economic or racial status, should be treated as a child of God whose life is of infinite value. When society or government penalizes any person for those or other reasons he/she should become the special object of the Church's concern.

A) Specifically, the denial to Communists of civil liberties held precious by the rest of the population should trouble the conscience of the Church until those liberties are fully restored.

A genuine concern for the dignity or worth of all persons, including Communists, will have its effect on the world scene. Harrison Salisbury in the February 6, 1962, *New York Times* reported the very real conflict in the Soviet Union between "a broadly based group of 'liberals'" and a neo-Stalinist group "for the dominant role of the country's future." Salisbury described the impact of Western ideals upon this group of "liberals." "As an example of the thinking characteristic of this group three recent events have shocked the members deeply. The first was the resumption of nuclear testing by the Soviet Union. The second was the invasion of Goa by India. *The third was the legal action taken by the United States against the Communist Party.*" Salisbury explains why each action "violated the ideals that the liberals had attributed to the three countries." With respect to the United States, *"They had believed that American democracy would respect the rights of even the most objectionable minority."* (emphasis added)

All too often we underestimate the power of attraction which policies based on respect for personality have for peoples of different religious and political convictions. Similarly we underestimate the disillusionment when we betray the image we have so carefully built over the years.

B) A second point where the Church should make a clear affirmation of its respect for personality is the war system. The church should be an unarmed instrument of love, protesting preparation for war against our brothers around the world, opposing the testing of nuclear weapons that admittedly cause illness and death to unpredictable numbers, and demonstrating our primary concern for persons in missions of mercy to Cuba, China, and other countries that have been the object of our

106

economic and political reprisal. While millions of Chinese are starving and millions of dollars worth of food lies idle in American granaries, the Church is sinning against its Lord and betraying the nation whose conscience it ought to be.

In pressing for programs that meet human need or affirm the value of personality, Christians must be aware of the problems and complexities that governments face in attempting, for example, to provide food for a nation that has been known to use grain as an instrument for foreign exchange or other governmental advantage. The Church, however, must not be deterred by such problems. Governments, which rarely if ever engage in pure acts unmuddied by ambiguities, are accustomed to negotiation and compromise. The role of the Church in this instance is not one of providing excuses for governments but of prophetically calling for the meeting of human need.

IV. Christians should seriously consider how we might encourage change within the Communist world. Without suggesting a detailed analysis of how our actions affect the Communist world let us set forth these considerations:

A) There is some evidence that in a number of the Communist nations there are what we might call hard Communists and soft Communists. These latter are much more ready to revise and modify Communist doctrine and practice. In Poland, for example, it was these Communists and not any anti-Communist group that launched and carried through the Polish Communist revolution against Khrushchev. We need to ask what it is that we might do that will strengthen the hand of the soft Communists and what it is that we now do that strengthens the hard Communists.

B) We need to ask ourselves whether totalitarianism in the Soviet Union and China is an inevitable result of Marxist doctrine or whether there are non-doctrinal reasons that in part created and sustain it. In Japan during the Meiji reformation, the Japanese government wanted to industrialize but had no capital for capital development. She took it from the backs of the peasants and turned it over to industrialists. In China and Russia there was a similar inability to get capital from the West. Taking it from the Chinese and Russian peasants could only be done by totalitarian and violent methods. Therefore our economic hostility to Russia and China has intensified the political totalitarianism we deplore.

Similarly, external danger from a great power like the United States provides both justification and rationale for concentration on development of heavy rather than consumer industry as a basis for manufacture of weapons. This whole preoccupation with defense and military matters has often resulted in greater internal controls and purges of those suspected of being friendly to the West, just as was true during the McCarthy period in the United States of those suspected of being friendly to Communists. It also subordinates education to science and technology as the way to become militarily superior to the West. The consequent relative illiteracy of the Soviet people when it comes to the humanities and the social sciences is another factor impeding tendencies toward democracy in the Soviet Union. There are other policies and actions of the United States which by and large receive the support of American Christians that, if changed, would also contribute to change in the Communist world.

Harrison Salisbury in the February 6, 1962 *New York Times*, points out how American actions influence life and thought within the Soviet Union. "It cannot yet be determined whether the neo-Stalinists or the liberalizers will win the struggle in the Soviet Union. Some Soviet citizens believe that international events may decide the issue. A relaxation of tensions would play into the hands of the liberals. A hardening of lines would produce a tightening reaction within Soviet society."

In suggesting that change in the Communist world may be dependent on changes in our part of the world, there is a certain amount of the pragmatic or of political estimation in this analysis. But much more basic is the thought that we must repent of our share in causing the evils that created and sustain totalitarianism. Repentance viewed in the political context denies the current popular idea that evil is incarnate in Communism and that the United States somehow represents the good. It means that the evil in our adversaries is somehow related to the evil in us and in our organization of society and that constructive change here is the precondition for constructive change there.

Repentance on our part will also have an impact on the non-Communist and especially the underdeveloped world, for it is our injustices and inequalities that have played a major role in strengthening and expanding Communist movements throughout the world. To some degree and on some issues such as colonialism and racial discrimination, many Christians have shown signs of repentance. But the death knell of colonialism and the ending of segretation have come largely as a result of the revolts of those who have been denied freedom. The Christian Church in America is still divided by caste and color. Where Western Christians have opposed colonialism, they have all too often remained silent about economic imperialism or military missions which have become effective substitutes for colonial rule. There has also been little evidence of repentance for the extremes of wealth and poverty around the world.

At the point of preparation for destroying our enemies and the hatred on which much of this preparation depends there is virtually no sign of repentance. We have not even repented of our use of nuclear weapons on Japanese cities. When one of our Marxist adversaries takes the initiative in proposing total world disarmament, there is no national will or significant Christian conviction which even insists on serious negotiations.

In reference to American Christians, Robert Hutchins remarked some years ago that we are an unrepentant lot. "We are not seeking so much to be good as to be powerful so as to force other nations to be good so that then it will be safe for us to be good." The chief problem we confront in this respect is that instead of seeking to be obedient to God and relying only on methods that are consistent with love, many Christians have assumed that Christian responsibility meant responsibility for the success of our particular nation state as the bearer of democratic values and hence values that serve Christian purposes. The Marxists act in reference to their Party and state in much the same way. If, however, as Paul Tillich has suggested, the real world conflict is between the Kingdom of God and the kingdom of evil rather than between nations or empires, then this conflict continues in spite of the rise and fall of nations. The Church rather than the nation is then the real bearer of the meaning of history. Its effectiveness is determined by its obedience to Christ rather than by its ability partially to control and manipulate secular political units. Nevertheless in its obedience to its Lord, the Church will also serve the state if it continually reminds the state of its sins and calls it to repent.

The Church must not limit its call to repentance to the verbal level. The clearest call is one of social action. Christians should themselves do the things which they call upon the state to do. A racially integrated church, for example, is more eloquent than a segregated church in seeking government support for racial equality. In the final analysis, the Church can be an effective answer to the human need that gave rise to Marxism only if the Church has a greater passion to change the world. This passion must manifest itself in movements for drastic social change. Christians will not only engage in sit-ins, freedom-rides, and bus boycotts but will act on a host of issues because they have a comprehensive concern.

V. Christians must also face the fact that a world-wide Marxist movement can be challenged only by a world-wide Christian church. Most Christians today do not look forward to a period such as the Middle Ages when an institutional Church was the dominant and hence unifying factor in civilization. We do nevertheless seek a manifest unity of spirit and purpose among Christians throughout the world that will, among other things, influence the political and economic and social fabric of every continent. This ecumenical church which is truly supranational will function in a religiously pluralist world as well as in a world of conflicting and competing secular political and economic systems. It will have world influence in proportion to its demonstrated concern for human need and its own refusal to seek special privilege or institutional advantage. It will also influence local and national life through the contributions of thought and witness made by Christians from other traditions and nations.

Sometimes opposition to Marxism is given as the rationale for Christian unity. Although the Marxist challenge may be one way of sharpening the need for a united Church, the only sufficient basis is Christian brotherhood and sisterhood in the service of one Lord.

VI. A further responsibility of Christians is to know Marxists as persons and engage in dialogue with them. In present-day America as well as in Marxist lands this presupposes a certain amount of daring. Fruitful dialogue also involves or should involve an understanding of Marxism, its weaknesses and failures. Many Marxists both in the United States and abroad are hungry for such conversation. On a number of occasions I have had the privilege of such dialogue with American Marxists and on two extended occasions with Russian officials. Individuals vary, but in each of these instances such subjects as civil liberties, race relations, war and peace, non-violence, economics, the "rightness or wrongness" of the crushing of the Hungarian revolution were topics of primary interest from which one moved to more basic ethical and religious questions.

It is quite possible to remain an anti-Communist while engaging in dialogue with Communists. One's opposition to Communism thereafter is more intelligent if it is conditioned by an appreciation for the motivation and idealism of the devoted Marxist. One root of the irrational and anxious anti-Communism of the right-wing extremists in America is their failure ever to have met or known a Communist. These extremists share with many American Christians a picture of Communists, including Communist thought and action, that does not accord with reality. This is not to suggest that the Communist problem ceases to be a problem if we know individual Party members. Actually Christians are better able to engage in dialogue and to win the respect of Marxists if they do not gloss over the very serious ethical, philosophical and practical problems inherent in Marxism.

Dialogue is not always planned. It happens whenever Christians and Communists confront each other as such. It can happen in a street meeting in New York or on a subway, on a college campus, or in Washington after a hearing before the House Un-American Activities Committee, or in prison when Christian conscientious objectors meet Communists imprisoned under the Smith Act.

Dialogue involves honesty and truth rather than pleasant words used to avoid offense or designed to persuade others that you are a "good guy." Nor is there any need to prove one's commitment or willingness to act by becoming involved in any current project which the Communists are promoting. Proof of one's commitment flows from inner integrity and action already taken in harmony with conviction.

VII. As a general rule, Christians should not engage in organizational collaboration or united front activity with Communists. There are at least five reasons for this. A) Such activity, however admirable the specific goal of the movement, is intended to serve more general Party purposes, such as building Party membership or using the names or participation of intelligent or prominent non-Communists to involve less astute persons and start them down the Marxist road. B) The goal of the united front is not only less important than it seems but is often obscured by questionable tactics and unethical action. C) The united front, while often seemingly democratic, is in fact controlled by strategically placed office workers and highly disciplined Party members who make the real decisions in harmony with predetermined Party policy. D) Participation in such Party fronts does not give a non-Communist any influence with the Party or its individual members. More often, collaborating non-Communists are looked upon as naive or as useful tools. If a Marxist has a problem about his activity or personal life or party involvements that he does not want to discuss within the Party, he never goes to the naive or the "tools" but to those whose sympathetic understanding and clear-cut non-Communist position have earned his respect. E) Above all, collaboration with Marxists obscures the Christian's social action witness which ought to be a testimony to one's whole faith as well as aimed at specific goals.

VIII. Finally, Christians have a responsibility to evangelize, to win Marxists to Christ. Such evangelism will take many forms. Johannes Hamel, a Protestant pastor, in his book, *A Christian in East Germany*, points out that

> a handful of Christians forces hundreds to take a decision, when these Christians do not try to hide from other people the gospel they believe. I have often been there as one or more Christians dealt openly with the political questions which burn our consciences — before hundreds of students, bringing the group to a decision and making the area of justice and freedom a little wider than before (p. 27).

Hamel also writes of Christians who begin

> to talk to half and full Marxists with love. With love — that means undiplomatically, in all frankness and freedom, yet not self-righteously or moralistically. And almost everywhere that happened we saw that the evil spirits stole away and the sea became still. In the place of their

111

dialectically grounded desire to liquidate us (for the moment largely in rhetoric) came human respect and the assurance that they wouldn't do us any harm because we were really "good honest people" whom one protects and defends. Then here and there something quite different occurred. Suddenly the mask, which looks so deceivingly like a real face, fell and revealed a helpless man who sinks under his load of sin and guilt, and who clings to the Christian who has treated him with a bit of love, who hasn't lied to him like the others. I have been in meetings where all the signs promised storm, and one held one's breath: will there be an explosion? And lo, it not only went well, but the political meeting transformed itself into a brotherly talk around the question of God's grace and commandment. (pp. 25-26).

In the United States over a period of many weeks during 1956 and 1957 five members of the Fellowship of Reconciliation met with five leading Communists. The meetings had come about as a result of two public debates and a number of incidents where these F.O.R. members had dramatically defended the civil liberties of Communists. As a result of this combination of concern for them as persons, action on their behalf, and friendly discussion, three of the group decided to leave the Communist Party. One of these men, John Gates, the former editor of *The Daily Worker*, wrote in his book *The Story of an American Communist:*

A few people, including Mrs. Roosevelt, Norman Thomas, and A. J. Muste, did support amnesty for us. These particular personalities had been staunch defenders of civil liberties throughout the years. But even here something bothered me. If any people were justified in not coming to our defense, it was just these three whom I have named. Had we not heaped personal and political abuse upon them . . . ? I asked myself how we would have responded had the situation been reversed, and my answer was not a comforting one. I came to feel that these individuals must have a moral superiority over us, that there must be something decidedly wrong with the attitude of communism toward democracy (p. 142).

In this instance an appeal for amnesty, out of concern for civil liberties for Communists, was the first step in a process that led three men out of the Party.

These brief illustrations do not encompass the subject, nor is it intended to suggest that the effort to evangelize is easy or always successful, or that the results are even known to those who have been in dialogue with Communists.

The point of such illustrations is to remind us that Christian love in action is relevant in areas where many Christians have resigned themselves to enmity and social distance. Perhaps we ought also to remind ourselves how much we gain as well as give in such encounters with Communists. Christian truth is not simply knowledge of a revelation once made but is existential in the sense that genuine encounter with those who are a part of God's present judgment will also expose us to truth.

Conclusion

In conclusion we must acknowledge the fact that in every Marxist land the committed members of the Communist Party are a minority. The great bulk of the people and even many of the Party members have acquiesced in totalitarianism but have not embraced it. More than a hundred million members of the Christian Church in the Soviet Union and Eastern Europe, together with those of other religious faiths, are evidence that materialism does not hold unchallenged sway even within its own citadel. It is well to recognize the price which many of these people have already paid in holding to their faith contrary to the wishes of a totalitarian government. Such courage and such integrity may play an additional role as history unfolds.

George Kennan in his *American Diplomacy* pins his hope for change inside the Communist world on a society which by contrast with Russia's is so good that it will be the incentive for those people to change their own society. He wrote during Stalinist days of his "faith that if the necessary alternatives are kept before the Russian people in the form of the existence elsewhere on this planet of a civilization which is decent, hopeful and purposeful, the day must come — soon or late, and whether by gradual process or otherwise, when that terrible system of power . . . will be distinguishable no longer as a living reality. . . ."

Although Kennan writes solely in terms of a political witness, much of what he says is applicable to Christian witness as well. He answers the question as to how a witness made thousands of miles away could have influence within the Soviet Union by saying: "In the lives of nations the really worthwhile things cannot be hidden."

Then he quotes Thoreau:

There is no ill which may not be dissipated, like the dark, if you let in a stronger light upon it . . . If the light we use is but a paltry and narrow taper, most objects will cast a shadow wider than themselves.

He concludes:

Conversely, if our taper is a strong one, we may be sure that its rays will penetrate to the Russian room and eventually play their part in dissipating the gloom which prevails there.

XV

The War in Vietnam

(*Concern*, December 1, 1964)

The first concrete evidence of American interest in extending the war to North Vietnam occurred last July. On July 31, South Vietnamese naval vessels shelled two islands off North Vietnam's shore, while two American warships were in the vicinity. This Gulf of Tonkin incident was discussed in the United States Senate on August 5, 6, and 7 by Senator Wayne Morse (D, Ore.).

Morse said:

> "The United States was connected with . . . the sending of South Vietnamese naval boats, boats that we supplied, that we armed, and whose crews were trained by the United States, to conduct the bombardment against the two North Vietnamese islands some 3 to 5 more miles off the coast of North Vietnam. We had American naval vessels in the vicinity . . . they were a provoking element. There is no questin that one of them was within the 12-mile limit of North Vietnam at the beginning of the bombardment" (*Congressional Record*, p. 20291).

There is some question as to whether the commanders of the American destroyers had advance knowledge of the South Vietnamese raids. Senator Morse, in comment on this, pointed out that American advisers in Saigon knew of the raids on North Vietnam by the South Vietnamese Navy but did not notify the U.S. Seventh fleet, which had ships in those waters.

Morse also said that in any event the presence of American warships in an area "where they could have given protection, if it became necessary" was bound "to be looked upon by our enemies as an act of provocation." North Vietnam did react by sending torpedo boats toward the destroyer.

I

The Providence, Rhode Island, *Journal* reported that the Maddox, one of the U.S. destroyers, "actually fired both warning shots and shots directed at the North Vietnamese craft before the PT boats launched their torpedoes or fired their guns. A Navy Department spokesman has confirmed this interpretation of the chronology . . . The U.S. warships opened fire while the craft, 'whose apparent intention was to conduct torpedo attack' (quotation is from a Navy release) were still at least 5000 yards — nearly three miles — away.

". . . Three miles is within torpedo range, we are told, but it's a long shot for a torpedo boat, especially for attack against something as maneuverable as a destroyer."

"Even on the thesis that the Maddox was justified in initiating action, it is still not correct to say she 'returned' the fire of the PT boat. *We started the shooting.*" (Providence, R. I. *Journal* reprinted in *Congressional Record*, August 21, 1964, p. 20291. Italics supplied.)

Following the incident in Tonkin Bay, President Johnson ordered reprisals in spite of the fact that U.S. warships were not damaged, while several of the North Vietnamese boats were destroyed in the action. The reprisals included sixty-four bombing sorties over four bases and an oil depot in North Vietnam and resulted in the destruction or damage of as many as twenty-five PT boats.

II

There was virtually no protest within the United States about the reprisals. Such aggression against another state could take place because the American people have been told again and again by our military leaders that troops from North Vietnam have been infiltrating the South.

In actuality there has been no such infiltration. Senator Morse said in the Senate, "I have been briefed many times, as have the other members of the Foreign Relations Committee, and all this time witness after witnesses from the State Department and from the Pentagon have admitted under examination that they had no evidence of any foreign troops in South Vietnam from North Vietnam, Red China, Cambodia, or anywhere else" (*Congressional Record*, August 5, 1964, pp. 17551-2).

In spite of this lack of evidence, an Associated Press dispatch from Tokyo reported in Kansas City papers of September 29 that "A high American source said yesterday, however, that U.S. contingency plans include possible bombing of infiltration staging areas in North Vietnam . . ."

"The same source also said the war against the Communists in South Vietnam could be ended within a few months if the infiltration from the North were stopped."

It is pure fantasy to assume that bombing the North Vietnamese will end the war in the South. That war is in large part directed against domestic repression and American intervention. As Senator Morse pointed out, "There is no freedom in South Vietnam . . . We are defending General Khanh from being overthrown. We are defending a clique of military generals and their merchant friends who live well in Saigon and who need a constantly increasing American military force to protect their privileged position" (*Congressional Record*, p. 17550).

Morse added that "four hundred thousand to 450,000 South Vietnamese military troops have been unable to defeat 25,000 to 35,000 — to use their top figure — Vietcong."

III

The July 30 New York*World Telegram and Sun* said the war in Vietnam was costing the United States $1.5 million a day. The *New York Times* of October 14 reported that U.S. economic aid to South Vietnam this fiscal year (July 1, 1964 to June 30, 1965) is expected to be worth $300 million, an increase of $60 million over last fiscal year. "Military aid this year is expected to total $206 million, not including the expenses of the military advisory mission."

The same edition of the *New York Times* quoted Secretary of the Army Stephen Ailes as saying, "Our casualties in killed and wounded in the Army alone have amounted to 900 men in the last year." United States Army men in South Vietnam number between 10,000 and 12,000 while the total Army, Navy, Air Force, and Marine personnel is about 19,500.

This war in Vietnam is an American war. When General Nguyen Khanh was asked, after he assumed the Presidency, about possible changes in the relationship between his government and the U.S. military he replied, "Everything we do, we do in very close cooperation with the American authorities" (*New York Times*, August 17, 1964).

Aviation Week and Space Technology on July 20, 1964, stated, "Mr. McNamara's war in Vietnam has been a failure. Now President Johnson has turned to a combat-tested veteran, General Maxwell Taylor, to try his hand from the field instead of the Pentagon."

The real architect of American military policy in Vietnam is General Taylor. The *Manchester Guardian* of August 13, 1964, said, "The American presence is incorporated in an Army which is being built up from 16,000 under General Maxwell Taylor, who used to be Chief of Staff. The situation is distorted and language debased by calling these troops advisers and their commander-in-chief ambassador."

IV

The average soldier who is sent to South Vietnam would prefer to remain at home in America. But one reporter writing from South Vietnam maintained that "the professional soldiers are positively gleeful at this chance to advance their professional status."

In an article in the August 24 *Nation*, Daniel Ford wrote: "A man must see combat before he is truly a soldier. Our World War II veterans are middle-age desk soldiers now and even our Korean veterans are in their thirties and passing beyond the stage where they might be leading platoons and companies in a future war. Thus there is a very human desire on the part of the U.S. Army to exploit the chaos in Southeast Asia to train a new generation of combat-experienced soldiers."

Undoubtedly there are other reasons, such as the fear that a negotiated truce or neutralization would erode away the U.S. military position in Southeast Asia, leaving only the Navy and aircraft based on Formosa, Okinawa, as the American presence in the Far East.

There is undoubtedly a psychological factor, such as would be involved in any discussion of how to pull American troops out of South Vietnam without causing too great a loss of prestige and dismay among anti-communist forces in Asia.

Probably the reason the United States continues in South Vietnam is a combination of many reasons. But among them is the hope of saving Southeast Asia for a Western, and from a Chinese, sphere of influence. This hope will probably be more difficult to realize now that China has exploded an atom bomb. That bomb serves notice on all Asian countries that China is and intends to be the great Asian power whose will cannot be thwarted with impunity.

Yet the Chinese A-bomb could also contribute to the ending of the war if the U.S. were at all open to neutralization. The North Vietnamese do not want Chinese domination, and the Chinese A-bomb is obviously another warning that China will not lightly give up expansion of her sphere of influence southward.

The November 7, 1963 *New York Times* reported that Eastern European diplomats believe North Vietnam would agree to President DeGaulle's proposal to unite North and South Vietnam if there would be a signed guarantee by the U.S., the U.S.S.R., France, Britain, and China to underwrite the neutrality of such a reunited nation and to protect it "against interference from Peking, Moscow, or Washington."

V

The United States is unlikely to take advantage of any such possibility, because of division in the White House. James Reston reported that "division is between those Johnson aides who want to expand the war into Communist North Vietnam with the direct participation of U.S. troops, and those who believe the risks of such a policy outweigh the advantages." He added, "It is even possible now to hear officials of this government talking casually about how easy it would be to 'provoke an incident' in the Gulf of Tonkin that would justify an attack on North Vietnam . . ." (*New York Times,* October 2, 1964).

On October 10, 1964, the *Kansas City Star* reported a dispatch from

117

Saigon which said, "Recently in the face of political deterioration in Saigon, there have been reports that Washington's reluctance to expand the war had weakened."

The same paper also reported that "President Johnson had reiterated several times in recent weeks that he does not favor a big offensive against North Vietnam."

Earlier in the year James Reston reported, "President Johnson is not likely to leave the Vietnamese problem where it is." He "is not likely to go on paying out more than $1 million a day to perpetuate a stalemate. Accordingly we are probably coming to the end of the period when the United States would neither fight nor negotiate." And we are probably approaching a new phase "where both fighting and negotiating will be stepped up" (*New York Times,* January 31, 1964).

The difficulty with this military strategy of stepping up the fighting is that it may not result in negotiations or in those that would be acceptable to the United States. The U.S. miscalculated in Korea. It could do so again. But the next few weeks or months will be crucial in the formulation of American policy.

XVI

Conscience and The Draft

(The Christian Century, June 28, 1967)

If the mood of Washington is indicative, the prospects for recognition of nonreligious objection to war are not good.

America's current conscription law provides that a person "who by reason of religious training and belief is conscientiously opposed to participation in war in any form" may, as an alternative to military duty, perform "civilian work contributing to the maintenance of the national health, safety or interest."

According to figures released by the Selective Service office in December 1966, there were 5,148 conscientious objectors then performing alternative service, the largest number in that category since the present law was adopted. During 1966, the total number classified as conscientious objectors — which includes those not yet assigned to alternative service — rose by about 1,000 to a total of 20,765. And during the past four years some 1,500 inductees have applied for conscientious objector status.

Thus the proportion of C.O.s to registrants has been steadily increasing. The Central Committee for Conscientious Objectors estimates that under the 1940 draft law it was one out of every 1,000 registrants; that from 1952 to 1962, under the present draft system, it was one to every 600 registrants; and that at present it is one out of every 350 to 400 registrants.

I

The draft law defines "religious training and belief" as "a relation to a Supreme Being involving duties superior to those arising from any human relations, but does not include essentially political, sociological or philosophical views or a merely personal moral code." Nevertheless, a small number of draftees who have stated that they do not believe in a "Supreme Being" have been officially recognized as conscientious objectors. This departure from the draft law's definition arises from the

119

U.S. Supreme Court's 1965 ruling, in United States v. Seeger, that conscientious objection does not depend on belief in a supreme being. The court declared: "The test might be stated in these words: A sincere and meaningful belief which occupies in the life of its possessor a place parallel to that filled by the God of those admittedly qualifying for the exemption comes within the statutory definition."

The Seeger case had been preceded by a number of requests to government for recognition of nonreligious objectors. For instance, in 1964 the Methodist General Conference stated:

> Christians cannot complacently accept rights or privileges accorded to them because of their religious views but denied to others equally sincere who do not meet a religious test. So long as military conscription legislation, remains in effect, we believe that all sincere conscientious objectors should be granted recognition and assigned to appropriate civilian service regardless of whether they profess religious grounds as the basis for their stand.

In April 1967 the Methodist Board of Social Concerns followed up the Seeger decision by asking Congress to provide "statutory recognition of moral, philosophical and humanitarian, as well as religious motivation for conscientious objection"— the same stand the National Council of Churches has taken two months before.

II

In addition to simple conscientious objection, however, a more specific kind of objection has developed. Since President Johnson escalated the war in Vietnam and the news reports of U.S. tactics there — napalm bombing, gas warfare, scorched earth operations and other procedures aimed at the civilian population — started coming through, a number of young men in the military have refused to fight in Vietnam. A celebrated case of this kind was that of the "Fort Hood Three"— Dennis Mora, a Puerto Rican; James Johnson, a Negro; and David Samas. For refusing to obey orders to embark for Vietnam, these men were sentenced to prison terms at hard labor — Mora to three years, Johnson and Samas to five years.

The three disobeyed orders because, they said, they regarded the Vietnam war as "illegal, immoral and unjust." Their request to a civilian court for an injunction against these orders declared that this war violates the Geneva accords of 1954, the United Nations Charter, the ruling on the Nuremberg judgments, and the United States Constitution. The court denied their plea, and they were appealing their case in a federal civilian court when they were arrested and sentenced by the army.

Other young men are reported to be in military prisons for similar objections to fighting in Vietnam. The army will not divulge figures, but my own estimate, on the basis of news reports and interviews with military men, of whom some have themselves served terms in military prisons, is that there are no fewer than 1,000 such objectors in military confinement. Some knowledgeable persons say there may be two or three times that many.

A third group is the "selective objectors," men who have not yet been drafted but have made it clear that they will not fight in Vietnam. Some of these might be called "just-war objectors;" they are prepared to fight in what they consider a just war (Vietnam being an "unjust war"). But most of them have never heard of the just-war doctrine and probably would not subscribe to it if they had.

Basically these men are existentialists; they make their decision in the face of the kind of war they are now confronting. If you ask them about World War II, they shrug their shoulders and agree that they might have been willing to fight then. But they weren't alive then or weren't old enough to have personal memories of that war. But, they add, such considerations are meaningless because they can conceive of only two probable patterns of warfare in the future: a nuclear, missile war between great powers; and a counterrevolutionary or imperialist war like that being waged in Vietnam. The August 10, 1966, *New York Times* described the existentialism of these "rebels" as nonideological: "It is not so much that they fight for causes as that they believe they must take responsibility, and they appear to feel responsible for a good bit. To allow yourself to be drafted is to take responsibility for Mr. Johnson's foreign policy. One must not cooperate with evil. That's what Eichmann did . . ."

The Methodist Board of Social Concerns, in the April 1967 statement referred to above, defended selective objectors: "Those who are conscientiously opposed to the war they are asked to fight are no less conscientious because they are unprepared to generalize about past or future conflicts which are irrelevant to the choice currently confronting them." In this case, too, the Methodist board took essentially the same position as that earlier set forth by the National Council of Churches General Board, whose February, 1967, statement asked statutory recognition "for those who are conscientiously opposed to a particular war, declared or undeclared, that is, to the one which a young person confronts at the time of induction." The N.C.C. board also called for "adoption of a new disciplinary provision for the person in armed service who cannot in conscience take part in the use of certain weapons or forms of warfare, or who cannot, in conscience, obey what is for him an unlawful or morally unacceptable order."

There is still a fourth category of conscientious objectors: men who have carried on nonviolent activities in connection with the civil rights movement. Some of them have become converted to nonviolence as a way of life. Others, believing that the U.S. government is not interested in freedom or justice for Negroes, are convinced that it cannot be working for freedom and justice in Vietnam. Both groups view the prodigal spending of lives and dollars in Vietnam as a betrayal of those Americans who, living in poverty and racial segregation, need the resources being wasted there.

III

The psychological mood of the United States is a factor to be noted in this connection. During World War II most Americans felt that our involvement was necessary and right. Compare the mood of those years with the mood of today, and it is clear that many Americans do not think that our involvement in Vietnam is morally defensible. When a nation is morally or psychologically in a state of doubt, some of its more sensitive citizens become conscientious objectors.

One more group of "conscientious objectors" to be considered is the men who are stigmatized as "draft dodgers"—a term I think most inappropriate. More than 4,000 young men have left the country to escape the draft. The reason for their flight is the same that prompted many of our forefathers to leave 19th century Europe. Our young men's departure is as much an indictment of U.S. militarism as our ancestors' flight was an indictment of European militarism. Some of them choose exile because they fear that, since they are not "religious" as defined by the law or are not opposed to all war, they will not be recognized as "conscientious objectors."

The typical American is likely to condemn these "escapees" for not staying to "face the music" or to help resist our Vietnam involvement. Surely we ought to be far more tolerant of positions different from our own, especially when they are taken under pressure by young, inexperienced men. In any case, history may prove that these young men chose as wisely as did those who fled European conscription a century ago.

One problem the war in Vietnam poses is how to view conscience. In 1940, Congress decided to legitimize opposition to war within the churches by recognizing religious objection to all war. Today it is the universities and the civil rights movement rather than the churches that have stimulated resistance to war. Because this nonreligious and nonpacifist objection is new and as yet unfamiliar, there is danger that the government and public opinion will refuse to acknowledge its validity.

Here two important questions need to be resolved: Shall we recognize that the conscience of the nonpacifist is as valid as that of the pacifist? Should the nonreligious objector to all or to a particular war be recognized? If the answer to these questions is No, the groundwork is laid for crushing the objector's dissent.

If the present mood of official Washington is indicative, the prospects are not good. The members of the Senate and House armed forces committees and General Lewis B. Hershey and other Selective Service officials are on record as wanting to put all such dissenters in prison. In a meeting on April 18, General Hershey went so far as to rebuke sharply a representative of the Unitarian Universalist group for asking that the words about "belief in a Supreme Being" be replaced in the draft questionnaire by a more inclusive terminology that would not exclude nontheists. Moreover, in a newspaper interview General Hershey gave a clue to his position on citizens who do not fit into the category of conscientious objector as now defined. "The man or woman who reserves the right to do nothing, who will not participate in a collective action of the United States," Hershey said, "shouldn't be around for the dividends" (*Kansas City Star*, April 19, 1967).

The unspoken corollary of Hershey's statements is a denial of the American tradition of relying on individual service freely rendered if and when the government decrees the necessity of military service. And it is unjust to suggest that those who resist compulsory service thereby become bad citizens, because they remain willing to serve their government in another capacity.

The most serious threat to conscientious objectors since World War I arose through the recent recommendation by the House Armed Services Committee that all conscientious objectors be inducted into the military before a decision is made concerning their eligibility for alternative service. They would then be subject to court martial. Committee Chairman L. Mendel Rivers of South Carolina, who is not known for his concern either for civilian control of the military or for civil liberties, thus endorsed further military domination of civilians and dissenters. The recommendation of his committee can be interpreted only as a direct effort to punish conscience and therefore as a direct insult to all the religious groups that are committed to support conscientious convictions. Fortunately, under pressure from, among other organizations, church groups concerned about the implications of the recommendation, Chairman Rivers had second thoughts and withdrew his committee's proposal on the ground that its effect would be to subject the "sincerely motivated people" of the peace churches to criminal prosecution for draft law violations.

One of the elementary principles of democracy is that dissenters are not to be turned over to the life-and-death control of those to whom they are objecting. Moreover, history proves that no country gains by attempting to coerce or crush the conscience of citizens who are so devoted to peace, freedom and justice that they are prepared to suffer

123

for their convictions. Coercion of conscience produces either resistance or apathy at a time when society can use and needs the contributions dissenters can make in other, nonviolent capacities. Beyond that, if society cannot tolerate dissent based on conscience, does it have the right to claim that it is free?

XVII

Draft Exiles in Canada

(The Christian Century, October 30, 1968)

Their motives are mixed, but we should not indict them as lacking understanding or courage or loyalty.

One of the most misunderstood of young Americans is the "draft dodger" (more appropriately called the "draft exile") — the young man who has gone to Canada to escape the draft. Just as many of our ancestors fled compulsory military training in 19th century Europe, so these young men, some with their families, have fled the United States today to take residence in Canada. For years we have praised those who rejected Napoleonic, Prussian, or other types of European militarism — but today's draft exile is accorded little praise. There is of course this difference: many of our ancestors fled conscription as such, whereas many who have gone to Canada have done so because they are unwilling to participate in a particular war, the war in Vietnam.

There are many more draft exiles in Canada than there are recognized conscientious objectors doing alternative service or draft resisters who have gone to prison. Because they are so numerous and because they are cut off from family, friends, church, and country, these exiles deserve the concern and support of other Americans. The problem lies at the door of the churches and of the unchurched "liberals," who before World War II fought to secure rights for religious objectors to all war but have not sought legal recognition of the nonreligious objector and the selective objector.

I

According to a survey by the Southern Ontario Committee on War Immigrants, approximately 15,000 male Americans of draft age have arrived in Canada since 1964 and have applied for landed immigrant status. These figures are based chiefly on Canadian immigration statistics but are supported by independent data. For example, the Toronto antidraft program handles nearly 20 cases each day. Ontario has the largest population of draft exiles, but there are also large groups in Montreal and Vancouver.

Before 1964, the number of Americans emigrating to Canada was increasing at a rate of about 1 percent per year. In 1964, the rate of increase was 7 percent, and in 1965, 21 percent, according to statistics in Canada's quarterly immigration bulletin. No one knows for certain how many emigrés are motivated by a desire to escape the draft. Neither are there any figures on military deserters. However, a knowledgeable informant whom I interviewed in Canada says that there are many such deserters, most of whom are "underground" and probably will not take up landed immigrant status until after the Vietnam war is over. Apparently, they are relatively safe, since so far the Royal Canadian Mounted Police has not cooperated with the F.B.I. in pursuing them.

The American draft exile, according to Jim Cairns of the Southern Ontario Committee on War Immigrants in Hamilton, Ontario, is "white middle class, liberal and college oriented." They are assisted almost entirely by Americans living in Canada. Almost all workers in the 23 antidraft programs or centers operating in Canada are themselves Americans or former Americans who feel an obligation to help others who want to resist the draft.

II

The results of a questionnaire published in *American Draft Exiles*, a sociological study by Robert Akakia, reveal that only 13 percent of the exiles are pacifists, although 44 percent are opposed to all types of war; the rest are for the most part selective objectors. One hundred percent described themselves as opposed to the war in Vietnam and 85 percent as opposed to the draft itself. Ninety-three percent indicated that they considered the U.S. the main aggressor in the war, and 56 percent that they believe the U.S. should be defeated. If these results, based on a sample of 200 draft exiles in the Toronto vicinity, are representative, they show that the draft exile is not a draft dodger in any usual sense but is ideologically motivated. The opening statement of welcome in the "Manual for Draft Age Immigrants to Canada," written by a Toronto lawyer, makes the same assumption: "Even though circumstances and not choice has made Canada your haven, we are happy to welcome you. Those of us providing service to the Anti-draft Programme assume that your opposition to the war in Vietnam stems from principle and that you are likely to become outstanding citizens."

The age range of draft exiles is 17 to 28, with 21.5 years the median. Their financial assets averaged $450 prior to immigration and $250 on arrival. "Contrary to popular myth," wrote Robert Akakia, "draft exiles are only slightly sympathetic to the hippie phenomenon. With respect to a control group survey of college seniors, draft exiles turn out to be relatively unsympathetic."

As to religion, answers to the questionnaire indicate that 37 percent consider themselves atheists (in the sense of not believing in a supernatural being); 22 percent are agnostic; 15 percent have a belief in God; and 26 percent view the question of the existence of a supernatural being as meaningless.

On its part, Canada has not officially opened its borders to young Americans of draft age, nor has it offered them political asylum. But since it has no draft law and is largely opposed to conscription, its policy is one of neutrality toward draft resisters. Thus General Mark Clark was simply denied his request when, on April 12, 1967, he asked the Canadian embassy in Washington to help return all the "draft dodgers." Again, Canadians in the antidraft programs are not trying to persuade Americans to flee the United States, although many of those Canadians think (as one antidraft executive put it) that "the U.S. is sick and becoming a military-oriented state." Their purpose is rather to assist young Americans who reached their own decisions and to make them feel welcome in Canada. A letter from a French-speaking citizen of Quebec published in a bulletin of the Montreal Council to Aid War Resisters states: "Many French-Canadians are anti-American, for many reasons, among which is economic domination. Therefore an American who is critical of his own government's behaviour usually merits the esteem of someone who himself is struggling for a greater degree of 'real liberty.'" As the manual of the Toronto group puts it: ". . . the toughest problem a draft resister faces is not how to immigrate but whether he really wants to. And only you can answer that. For yourself. That's what Nuremberg was all about."

Most draft exiles apply for "landed immigrant status"—that is, lawful admittance to Canada for permanent residence. A landed immigrant who has lived in Canada for any five of any eight years has acquired "domicile" and is eligible to apply for Canadian citizenship. Since Canada, unlike the United States, does not require aliens to register, a landed immigrant is not obliged to report periodically to the Canadian authorities. But those who, for one reason or another, consider landed immigrant status undesirable can enter Canada by obtaining a "student entry certificate," which is granted on a year-to-year basis and can be renewed.

Under the new immigration regulations of October 1967, visitors to Canada may apply for immigrant status or a student certificate after they have entered the country. Applicants qualify for immigrant status if they can compile 50 out of a possible 100 "assessment units." For example, a job offer counts for ten units; occupational skill, for ten units;

age status from 18 to 35 years, for ten units. Each successfully completed year of formal education and each year of apprenticeship or professional, vocational or other training brings one unit, up to a maximum of 20. Five units each are granted for ability to read, write, and speak English and French fluently. Even before 1967, about 70 percent of all draft exiles had no trouble in obtaining immigrant cards, according to Robert Akakia. Fifteen percent had some difficulty, and the other 15 percent "a great deal of difficulty." The new unit system makes the process still easier. College-trained people generally have no difficulty finding work, but high school boys have to hunt for unskilled jobs, though the antidraft committees usually are able to secure employment for them.

Apparently all who intend to become draft exiles must have a birth certificate or similar paper; a high school or college diploma; passport photos; and at least $250. Letters of recommendation and college transcripts have also proved helpful.

Landed immigrant status does not entail renunciation of American citizenship, and in fact the manual for draft age immigrants does not recommend such renunciation. For one thing, giving up one's U.S. citizenship before acquiring citizenship in another country simply means that one is stateless, with no rights to travel or re-enter the United States. Actually a small number of young draft exiles, after a year or more in Canada, have returned home — often because they want to witness publicly for their convictions against war.

IV

But the young men who have gone to Canada only after receiving their draft induction notices are obviously in violation of the law and cannot return to the United States — even for family emergencies — without risking imprisonment. When a draft exile's father died in 1967, two F.B.I. agents showed up at the funeral! Those, however, who can prove that they received landed immigrant status before the date of their induction notice may meet different treatment. Possibly, if they are granted Canadian citizenship before attempting return to the U.S., they will be dealt with like any other Canadian citizen; but there is no legal certainty in this regard.

The Toronto manual cited above points out that Canada is not the end of the world so far as schools, jobs, housing, etc., are concerned. "You do not leave civilization behind when you cross the border . . . the truth is that Canada is a nice place to be." To show that Canada is more than just a haven for people in trouble, the manual lists 35 universities, about a hundred occupations in strong national demand, and statistics which prove that Canada is ahead of the United States in standard of living, with more telephones, refrigerators, washing machines, cars, and TV sets per household than its neighbor.

In 1967, the Evangelism and Social Service Board of the United Church of Canada, Canada's largest Protestant denomination, voted an appropriation to help the draft exiles. Later, however, the church announced that the money would not be disbursed, since "it would imply interference in the affairs of another country." After a public controversy a number of ministers formed a committee and some congregations decided to "raise the money that the church as a whole had declined to contribute." Other aid has come chiefly from the Quakers and Unitarians and from university faculty and student groups.

The chief problem of the draft exile are loneliness and frustrated desire to return home to visit his family. Some also find it difficult to adjust to Canada's more conservative, formal culture. Yet these problems can be surmounted. Draft exiles generally indicate that the step taken in going to Canada is their first political act; it makes them think, and, like all dramatic acts, is a maturing process.

Exile for whatever reason should not be idealized or romanticized. Most young Americans who choose exile simply think it preferable to a possible five years in prison; some indeed are not sure that they have the inner strength to stand prison life. As I have discovered in counseling draft-age Americans, all drastic actions are motivated by a mixture of idealism, realism, courage, and fear. But no adult can indict these young men as lacking understanding or courage or loyalty. At 18 or 20, these qualities are at a different level than at 35 or 40. Exile today may be a mistake, but on the other hand it may be the door of opportunity and service, as it was for many Europeans in the 18th and 19th centuries who came by faith and necessity to an unknown land.

XVIII

Amnesty and Reconciliation

(*The Christian Century*, December 27, 1972)

Amnesty for war resisters has become a political issue in the United States, not only because the Vietnam war is highly unpopular but also because scores of thousands of Americans have openly protested against it. In addition to conscientious objectors, deserters from the military, and escapees from the draft, these thousands include men and women now in prison because of their participation in demonstrations or other antiwar activities. Their sympathetic families and friends easily number another million adults scattered throughout the nation. Obviously, this is a situation that cannot be ignored. Is amnesty the answer?

Articulate supporters of the war are insisting that "those who have violated the law should expect to be punished instead of being forgiven." On the other hand, most of the resisters insist that they have done nothing which calls for "forgiveness." *Amex-Canada* (published by Americans exiled in Canada) speaks for them in an editorial: "The real question is whether the tens of thousands of American youth in exile, in jail or in hiding would conceivably pardon the U.S. government, not the other way around." Which is to say that in their eyes it is our government that is the criminal in this war, not they.

All this, however, is to confuse amnesty with pardon or forgiveness. "Amnesty" comes from the Greek *amnestia*, which means not remembering, obliviousness, intentional overlooking. The Supreme Court stated the case clearly back in 1887: "A pardon relieves an offender from the consequences of an offense of which he has been convicted, while amnesty obliterates an offense before conviction and in such case, he stands before the law precisely as though he had committed no offense" (U.S. v. Bassett).

I

Forgiveness, then, implies a pardon given to a guilty person. But amnesty is reconciliation with persons who feel no guilt because their actions were ethically motivated. It is intended to heal a rupture in the body politic. One reason for the failure to distinguish between amnesty and forgiveness it that, in Christian thought, reconciliation is possible only if those who have alienated themselves from God by their own sinful actions acknowledge their guilt and ask the divine forgiveness, which they know is assured by a perfect God whose nature it is to love and to forgive. But in an alienation where neither party is perfect and neither will acknowledge guilt, reconciliation can take place only if one or both parties overlook their differences.

The opposite of amnesty is retribution, that is, punishment and revenge. However, punishment inflicted on persons who do not admit guilt has no value to them; it simply reinforces the unhealthy attitudes of hatred and revenge on the part of the punishers, and therefore leads to greater alienation instead of to reconciliation. Amnesty should be viewed as a procedure by which the government can undo what the government itself has done. In effect, the government must act as though healing the rupture is more important than perpetuating it. In the first place, government ought not to impose penalties, especially felonious ones, on persons whose offense is political. Essentially, a political offense is either a response to conscience or an exercise of the right of free speech intended to protest governmental policy or to achieve a change in government. Therefore, nonviolent opposition to government policies should be treated as different from crimes against persons or property.

Granted, government may impose penalties for resistance during a war; but following the war it ought to take steps to eliminate all disabilities connected with the political activity for which penalties were originally applied. Since societies can become or remain free only if political dissent is permitted, governments are not making a concession to political opponents when they grant amnesty so much as they are ensuring the continuance of vigorous democratic debate. Indeed, for a government to punish political offenders—e.g., to deprive them of the right to vote or run for office—is a sign of governmental insecurity.

The case for amnesty is especially strong in relation to the war in Vietnam. The 1964 presidential election was won by Lyndon Johnson on a no-war platform, and the 1968 election was won by Mr. Nixon on a clear pledge to end the war. Neither pledge was kept. Congress did not declare war yet continued to authorize personnel and funds for it. The small group in Washington who, in defiance of public opinion, made the decision to enter and escalate the war broke both moral and constitutional law. Draft resisters or military deserters may have been technically guilty of lawbreaking, but they were operating on a higher moral and legal plane than the officials who took the nation into the war.

Amnesty would erase the double standard of not prosecuting the various presidents, secretaries of state and defense, joint chiefs of staff and other top government officials for their crimes against humanity while prosecuting those whose offense was refusal to participate in a war that millions of Americans have adjudged immoral and illegal.

II

Those who object to amnesty, said *Newsweek* in interpreting a public opinion poll, generally contend "that an American should be willing to serve his country." If we accept this as a valid norm the question still remains. What constitutes service of country? Blind obedience to a commander-in-chief even when he adopts a policy that is contrary to the will of the governed? Or does serving one's country require a refusal to engage in acts that harm or threaten to destroy the U.S. or its reputation? Did the Germans who obeyed Hitler serve their country? Whatever one's opinion of the Nuremburg trials, in which the victors judged the vanquished, they resulted in wide acceptance of the idea that obedience to illegal or immoral orders is not the highest or even a valid form of service to country. Amnesty would restore to useful citizenship those whose disobedience to law helped their fellow Americans discern the true nature of the Vietnam war.

Some insist that there should be no amnesty because granting it would be disrespectful or unfair to the Americans who were killed, wounded, or made prisoners in Vietnam. This is the familiar device of pitting one group of victims against another in order to deny justice to both, on the assumption that if one group has been badly treated the other should be too. This argument leaves out of account the small group of men in the Eisenhower, Kennedy, Johnson, and Nixon administrations who made the decisions that have been proved wrong in Indochina. Those who would be amnestied, however, not only fought the moral battle against their own government but also participated in the political battle to end the war. Many of them suffered imprisonment, exile, loss of job, or other penalties, but they did contribute to decisions to bring ground troops home from Vietnam and hence to the lowering of casualties, and their actions were a continuing indictment of the air war and of Vietnamization.

Answering the argument that amnesty would be unfair, congresswoman Bella Abzug drew the following analogy: When our court system sentences a man to death and later strikes down the law under which he was condemned, reversal of the original sentence is ordered, that is, the courts do not insist that the offender be executed for the sake of consistency or of honoring those who were wrongfully put to death. Similarly, the fact that one group in Vietnam was treated unfairly should not prevent amnesty for another group. Justice requires restoring to useful citizenship those whose offense was resistance to a war now widely recognized as one we should never have embarked on.

American Legion spokesman oppose a blanket amnesty on the ground that it "would let all the so-called 'high-principled' off and with them it would let off all the 'low-principled'—the stickup men and wanted murderers who failed to register in order to flee justice." There is no evidence that robbers or murderers failed to register for the draft in order to avoid being caught. But if there are such, amnesty would apploy only to their political offense of resisting the war, not to their crimes of robbery or murder. A person's previous criminal record does not justify treating him differently on a different issue.

III

There are two approaches to blanket amnesty. American Legion spokesmen call for a case-by-case approach, under which some court or parole-type board will consider the total life record of each war resister. The model here is Harry Truman's three-man "Amnesty Board." This rejected Jehovah's Witnesses and other minority-group war objectors, with the result that very few of those who should have been actually were amnestied. As a matter of fact, a case-by-case approach undermines the whole idea of amnesty because it permits the persons in charge to reject any individual or group whose principles they object to. The three members of Truman's board, for instance, were all more or less "militarists." That board's chairman was also chairman of a Citizen's Emergency Committee for Universal Military Training, and of the two other members, one was police chief of Manchester, New Hampshire, and subsequently national commander of the American Legion, and one had waged a racist campaign for the governorship of a southern state.

The most popular alternative to blanket amnesty is conditional amnesty. Bills now pending in Congress would grant amnesty to all who agreed to do two or three years of alternative service. But those concerned see such conditions as punishment for their refusal to participate in an immoral war. Appropriately, the Legion objects to conditional amnesty. Its spokesmen point out that alternative service in a government agency such as a veterans' hospital would take jobs away from people who need them — for instance, from unemployed veterans of the Vietnam war. Moreover, they say that "the quality of service in VA hospitals and other agencies" would deteriorate if these were staffed with men who viewed "government service as a sort of punishment."

Finally, opponents of amnesty insist that it might lower the morale of our armed forces or discourage enlistments. But this is not a likely result. Certainly amnesties granted in the past have affected neither military morale nor number of enlistments. Indeed, a government that is concerned to heal the wounds of war and rectify injustice will probably inspire a higher morale than a government that seeks the last drop of blood from every citizen, in civilian or military life, who runs afoul of the law.

But what of the impact of amnesty on law and order? Would it encourage resistance to future wars on the assumption that amnesty would again be forthcoming? The question is inept. For one thing, there was no general amnesty after World Wars I and II or the Korean War. For another, the anmesties following the Civil War and the Spanish American War had no discernible causal impact on war resistance in the two world wars. In any case, the hope that amnesty will be granted following a war is hardly an incentive for resisting the government during a war, when the immediate penalty is imprisonment or exile.

The concern about law and order relates chiefly to crimes against persons or property. As stated above, political offenses are in a different category. If their civil rights were restored by amnesty to the people who refused to condone the massive violence in Vietnam, they would tend to be an influence in our society against violence and against a repetition of wars like the one in Indochina. On the other hand, conditioning a society to accept war and mass training in the techniques of military violence surely tends to encourage the spirit of violence. Amnesty at the hands of the President or of Congress for those who rejected both the massive violence of the Vietnam war and the illegal interference by one nation in the land of another would not imply that violence and infringement of others' rights were being honored.

IV

In 1868, when President Andrew Johnson proclaimed amnesty for those who had engaged in insurrection or civil war against the United States, he said:

> A retaliatory or vindictive policy, attended by unnecessary disqualifications, pains, penalties, confiscations and disfranchisements, now as always could only tend to hinder reconciliation among the people and national restoration, while it must seriously embarrass, obstruct and repress popular energies and national industry and enterprise.

The general thrust of that statement is as valid today as it was a century ago. The nation is more seriously divided today than at any other time since the Civil War — divided because of the war, which induces or aggravates a host of injustices: repressive policies against dissenters, economic deprivation due to military priorities, inflation, etc. Amnesty would not bring total healing. It would, however, be the requisite first step.

XIX

The U.S. Role in Asia's Future
Needed: An Imaginative Policy That Will Secure Peace in the Far East

(*The Christian Century,* September 29, 1976)

Most Americans have given little attention to U.S. Policy in the Far East. The end of the Vietnam war did not even precipitate a major debate about the part America could play in Asia's future. One reason for this failure to re-examine Asian policy is that detente with China seemed at least temporarily to dispose of a major enemy and hence of the need for reappraisal. Another and perhaps more fundamental reason is the widespread myth — carefully nurtured by political leaders and spread by the news media — that the war in Vietnam was, though mistaken, an honorable mistake. A typical characterization of the war is that made by Anthony Lewis, a *New York Times* columnist who had opposed the war but wrote afterwards: "The early American decisions on Indochina can be regarded as blundering efforts to do good. But by 1969 it was clear to most of the world — and most Americans — that the intervention was a mistake."

I

The future role of the U.S. in Asia is inevitably conditioned not only by America's defeat suffered in Vietnam but also by our interpretation of that defeat. The war in southeast Asia was not a mistake or a blunder; it was a natural by-product of a foreign policy rooted in the military-industrial complex, which defines the American way of life as monopoly capitalism plus military strength. Other evidence of this foreign policy thrust are the U.S. intervention in Chile, the invasion of the Dominican Republic, the bolstering of Brazilian and other Latin American dictatorships, the embargo against Cuba, support of now overthrown dictatorships in Greece and Portugal, and the Ford administration's efforts to involve the United States in Angola.

German military strategist Karl von Clauswitz helps our thinking at this point. He wrote:

There is a recurrent failure to realize that the fabric of history is woven upon one loom. The theory that makes an absolute distinction between war and peace is false. War is an overt expression of covert tensions and conflicts which exist in every stable and peaceful social situation. In war things that have been hidden become revealed.

The internal U.S. emphasis on ever-increasing business expansion and constantly increasing military budgets at the expense of the average tax-payer is related to the kind of foreign policy we have. The expanding size of the military budget — Congress has approved $112 billion for 1977 and the Pentagon is asking $130 billion for 1978 — is based not only on the economic assumption that major American industries must have military contracts to maintain profits but also on the military assumption that the United States might have to fight major wars in Asia and in Europe at the same time. The military assumptions, however, are rooted in economic needs — the need of American multinational corporations for political stability that eliminates the threat, whether communist or nationalist, that other countries may seize control over their own economies.

American foreign policy in the Far East prior to the war in Vietnam was directed by three major aims which continue to misguide us. The first is opposition to any nation or movement that would close the door to American business penetration of Asia. This aim was behind the "open door policy of the 1890s and 1900s. When communism became a force in Asia following World War II, the "open door" evolved into a policy of containment.

The second aim of U.S. foreign policy is to integrate as many Asian countries as possible into an American-dominated global system. That integration requires political, economic, and military dependence on the United States and the fitting of other nations' resources into the needs of American policy. Military bases in such places as Korea, the Philippines, Japan, Taiwan, Thailand, and Vietnam were all a part of this policy of dependence, as were the various economic agreements and military alliances, even with right-wing or military dictators such as Syngman Rhee, Chiang Kai-shek, General Nguyen Van Thieu, General Park Chung Hee and General Thanom Kittikachorn.

Third, American policy has aimed to maintain an armed presence around Asia in order to thwart communist — and especially Soviet — expansion in that continent. This policy, begun in the 1950s, is now temporarily accepted or tolerated by the Chinese, who also view the Soviet expansion as dangerous. To the U.S., detente maintains the *status quo*, securing for the time American power positions in Asia, and detente with both Russia and China subtly encourages Chinese-Russian rivalry (short of war), with the United States holding the balance of power.

II

The fact that U.S. Asian policy is bankrupt becomes clear if we look at three major areas where the United States intervened in pursuit of these policy goals. In the civil war in China, the U.S. rushed in on the side of Chiang Kai-shek and lost. No effort was made to change relations with mainland China until defeat in Vietnam virtually forced the U.S. to do so. Korea was the second disaster for American policy, beginning with the army's decision during World War II to have the Russians occupy North Korea — that is, to receive the surrender of Japanese forces in Korea north of the 28th parallel. General John Hodge, head of the U.S. occupation forces in South Korea, refused to cooperate with a non-communist Korean party — the Korean People's Republic — which could have unified Korea. Instead, the Korean People's Republic was destroyed, its leader was assassinated, and Syngman Rhee was imported from America to head a right-wing government which kept the country permanently divided. Then, during the Korean war, the best the U.S. armed forces could do was to secure a stalemate and shore up South Korea with American military might. During the 22 years that followed, the U.S. has spent roughly $11 billion to groom its garrison state in Korea and has provided since 1950 an additional $4 billion in military aid to the South Korean government. Instead of helping the creation of a unified non-communist Korea, U.S. policies are responsible for the continuing division of that country under left- and right-wing governments — and for making the Korean peninsula one of the most heavily armed regions in the world.

Vietnam struck the third major blow to U.S. foreign policy in Asia. The U.S. first tried to help the French regain colonial rule; after the French defeat, the U.S. installed a dictatorial puppet government in order to control Vietnam for American interests. The creation and support of U.S. client states, however, represents a foolish attempt to swim against the current of Asian nationalism, and it has produced the unanticipated result of arming the nationalists: 80 percent of the military equipment supplied to Chiang Kai-shek was lost to the Chinese communists, and an even greater percentage of the weapons sent to South Vietnam were lost to the North. As a result, a reunited Vietnam now has the best-equipped armed forces in southeast Asia — and could provide important military aid to guerrillas anywhere in the region.

III

The U.S. defeat, combined with Vietnam's new regional military superiority and China's looming presence, has brought on certain other setbacks to American foreign policy. The U.S.-sponsored Southeast Asia Treaty Organization (SEATO) has broken up. U.S. bases in Thailand were ordered to close and U.S. troops to withdraw by last March. President Ferdinand Marcos of the Philippines announced in July, 1975, that his government wanted to control U.S. bases there, maintaining that "there remains no reason why foreign troops should remain on our soil." Thailand has severed relations with Taiwan, and the Philippines has recognized China.

In view of the failure of past American policy in Asia, what is needed now is an imaginative policy that will win friends for the United States and also secure peace in the Far East. Such a policy should begin with seven assumptions:

• Abandoning its self-image as the world's policeman, the United States should seek to influence rather than to control international events.

• The U.S. must have positive goals instead of simply reacting to communism. Anticommunism is an inadequate basis for interpreting and dealing with world events, and there are also real differences among communist nations.

• The U.S. needs to move from reliance on military power to reliance on other methods such as diplomacy, and on other forms of power—political and economic.

• The U.S. must begin to compete with other great powers on a civilian level. Subversion and revolution cannot be opposed in Asia except by the development of a socioeconomic structure that is better than what totalitarian communism has to offer.

• The United States should be primarily concerned with assisting Asian nations to develop their own human and material resources, guided by their internal needs. The U.S. benefits both politically and economically when other nations are developed to the point where most of the people can make use of the products of American industry. But the U.S. will have to stop protecting, ensuring, and encouraging the expansion of multinational corporations; owing no loyalty to any one nation, they tend to serve their own narrow interests, thereby thwarting the self-development of Asian countries' resources.

• The U.S. should abandon executive secrecy and anything which denies Americans and their congressional representatives the information they need for participating in foreign-policy decisions, for examining proposed alternatives as well as rejecting some. Democracy works on the assumption that no foreign policy is adequate or appropriate if it does not have the support of the people.

• Finally, the aim of the United States must be that of demilitarizing the Far East—to avoid nuclear war and long, costly conventional or guerrilla conflicts, and to shift U.S. resources to civilian purposes.

If it is argued that the Soviet Union will replace the United States as the dominant military power in the Far East, there are a number of possible responses. One is to let the Russians do it, earning the hatred that comes from trying to divert the currents of nationalism; let their elite reap the consequences of expending resources and spreading manpower thin at the expense of the Russian people. Another possible response is to rejoice in the possibility that there may be forces within the Soviet Union and other communist countries which would welcome the chance to demilitarize and disarm if they no longer had to compete militarily with the U.S.

More specifically, there are a number of concrete steps the U.S. could take to turn around the disastrous foreign policy course of the past. In Korea the South has the fifth-largest army in the world, half of it experienced combat veterans of the Vietnam war, and a quite modern and varied air force—whereas the North has a smaller army, a much smaller reserve force, and only defensive interceptor aircraft. The United States could begin to pull out the hundreds of nuclear weapons it has in South Korea and shortly thereafter withdraw its troops. The House defense appropriations sub-committee has already recommended that by 1978 U.S. forces in Korea be reduced to 20,000—about half their June, 1976 strength. Making a case for the withdrawal of American ground forces from Korea but the retention of ships and naval air forces, the Center for Defense Information in Washington quotes U.S. Army Colonel Zeb Bradford:

> We have learned (from Vietnam) that, in strategic terms, ground power can be quite inflexible once committed, however much flexibility it may provide on a tactical level. . . . While aircraft and ships can often reverse course and make a clean break, ground forces rarely can do so, once engaged.

In southeast Asia, the United States should accept its defeat and begin to cooperate on reconstruction and trade with the governments of Vietnam, Cambodia, and Laos to achieve by civilian and economic means a good that it could not achieve by military strength. We can learn from Japan, which had to give up its goal of military and political control over Asia during World War II but which has gained economically what it lost militarily. Now either the chief trading partner of most Far East nations or second in rank, Japan has also engaged in economic gestures of goodwill such as building the bridge and highway which link up two of the Philippine Islands into a larger road system.

IV

The most important immediate step in Asian policy is to cement relations with China as soon as possible. The original agreement of detente provided that the U.S. would disengage from Taiwan soon after the Vietnam war ended. This means that the U.S. must abrogate the mutual security treaty and sever formal ties with Nationalist China. The invitation to revisit China last February issued to Nixon instead of to Ford or Kissinger must be understood as a warning, if not an implied criticism, for those who have failed to implement that agreement. If the U.S. continues to recognize Taiwan as China, the Chinese may in the post-Maoist period decide that it is more profitable to have an accommodation with Russia at the expense of the U.S.

In addition the U.S. should place a major emphasis on relations with the five governments of the Association of South East Asian Nations formed in 1967: Thailand, Indonesia, the Philippines, Malaysia, and Singapore. Along with helping them to build a higher standard of living within a strong socioeconomic structure, the U.S. would also have to phase out its military presence in the Philippines and encourage the restoration of basic civil liberties there and in Indonesia — two so-called "guided democracies."

The billions of dollars saved by demobilizing American troops in Korea and Thailand and dismantling bases in the Philippines could be used to help southeast Asian countries develop resources and improve standards of living. For example, the United States could assist in the rural electrification of these countries, building hydroelectric plants to harness the tides and rivers and encouraging the formation of locally-owned cooperatives to produce and distribute the new power. Above all, the United States should not seek to impose its approach to development but should cooperate with Asians in their programs. We must, furthermore, be aware that any socioeconomic structure that will serve as a genuine alternative to totalitarianism cannot be monopoly capitalism, exploiting the land and people for the benefit of a handful of stockholders back in the States.

Economist Terence McCarthy has estimated that if no military expenditures had been made by nations after the communist victory in China,

the realizable wealth of the world (in the form of housing, hospitals, schools and universities, productive facilities, developed infrastructures including electric power and transportation, plus agricultural potential) would have been at least 50 percent higher than it is today.

The Vietnam war was purchased for $150 billion, money that the U.S. could have spent to end poverty and malnutrition in the Philippines. A democratized Philippines could have become an Asian showcase of a viable political and economic alternative to dictatorship. World poverty, McCarthy writes, "is not an excess of population over potential means of subsistence, but the displayed preference of peoples to spend on arms what should be spent on the short-range welfare and the long-range productive capacity of mankind." The key to human resource development and to human freedom is demobilization and disarmament. Seeking these for the good of Asia's future could turn the

U.S. away from the past pattern of dishonorable "mistakes" like the Vietnam war — and other Far East ventures, military as well as economic — and toward the seeking of an honorable peace.

XX

The Case Against the C.I.A.

(*Fellowship*, December, 1976)

The first issue is military: the Central Intelligence Agency is the President's secret military establishment, with which he can unilaterally make war anywhere in the world. The Senate Select Committee on Intelligence Activities has reported that the CIA not only engages in paramilitary operations but that these occasionally have involved "combat activities" and hence "frequently amount to making war . . ." This secret power to make illegal war is maintained to keep Congress and the American people from examining and debating crucial areas of foreign policy.

A former CIA official, Harry Rositzke, wrote in *The Washington Post*:

> The President and the Secretary of State were convinced that the Congress would not agree with their Angolan policy and would not supply the required funds. Secret funds provided the easy way out. The use of covert actions, not to achieve a foreign purpose in secret but to evade Congressional scrutiny, degrades the covert instrument into a domestic political tool.

The Senate Committee asserted that these covert CIA operations have sometimes been used "simply because the agency is less accountable to the public" than the armed forces, whose military operations are "highly visible."

This means that the CIA has now become the chief instrument by which the United States provokes or precipitates a war. Despite frequent press reports of CIA action in Asia, Latin America, the Middle East, and Africa, the President and the Congress have continued to conspire, through the secret carte blanche allocation of funds, in the CIA's operations.

The Senate Committee now recommends that "any covert use by the U.S. Government of American citizens as combatants should be preceded" by notification to Congress with the understanding that "Congress should be empowered to terminate such use at any time." Significantly, this Senate intelligence committee is not asking that the CIA or the President seek permission from Congress to engage in acts which may precipitate war, but only the power to terminate such combat. It is far more difficult to mobilize Congress to stop an action overseas than it is to persuade Congress to authorize it in the first place. Perhaps this is the reason the Constitution does not give the Congress a veto on the Presidential power to declare war but gives Congress alone the power to declare war.

A second basic issue in the current discussions about the CIA and the other intelligence agencies is secrecy: does the public have a right to know what the CIA and the government in general are doing? The case for secrecy is based on the desire to keep important information from becoming available to potential or actual enemies. In actuality, the Soviet Union and other nations are well informed about CIA covert activities. When the Chairman of the House Select Committee on Intelligence, Otis Pike, asked the Director of Central Intelligence if the "Soviets know what our intelligence effort is," William Colby responded that "they know a good deal about it . . ." (One of the items the CIA wants kept secret is its budget and spending. But the House Committee report said: "What is clear is that the Russians probably already have a detailed account of our intelligence spending, far more than just the budget total. In all likelihood, the only people who care to know and do not know these costs today are American taxpayers.")

The Senate Committee indicated that it is virtually impossible for the CIA to keep its overseas activities secret. "Almost every operational act by a CIA officer under cover in the field — from working with local intelligence and police to attempting to recruit agents — reveals his true purpose and chips away at his cover." It is now clear that the CIA actions in Angola were widely known in Africa and a number of Administration sources have indicated that the secret U.S. aid and its escalation sparked the Soviet intervention. The Center for National Security Studies in Washington, D.C. said: "The CIA intervention in Angola is not a secret to the combatants there, to the leaders of other African countries, or to the USSR. The primary victims of secrecy are the Congress and the American people."

What then, should be public policy?

The Congress should forbid U.S. intelligence agencies from engaging in covert actions or classifying as secret information on budget, the presence of U.S. military or paramilitary forces in other countries, military or other aid to foreign countries, the training of insurgent movements, and the like. The board of directors of the American Civil Liberties Union, after extensive study and debate, adopted a policy statement which lists only two types of information which could properly be kept secret without violating the public's right to know. These are "technical details of military operations or weaponry, knowledge of which would be of benefit to another nation," and "military contingency plans with respect to foreign powers, but not with respect to surveillance of domestic activity."

If it is argued that the CIA needs secret agents in other countries for espionage, one response given by former intelligence officials is that such agents provide only five to ten percent of the raw data, are suspect as double agents or are doubted for other reasons. The information is not very useful unless the information can be confirmed by other means (such as satellite photography, communications and other electronic intelligence, speeches, and published articles). Herbert Scoville, the CIA's former Assistant Director for Scientific Intelligence, said that "unless the information" secured by spies or human agents "could be confirmed by other means, it might well be ignored." He added that covert agents "rarely provide useful intelligence in the military area. It is hard enough to recruit an agent who has any inside knowledge on military affairs, but it is even more difficult to recruit one who has sufficient technical background to provide timely and meaningful information on the characteristics of modern weapons."

Morton Halperin, former Deputy Assistant Secretary for National Defense and senior staff member of the National Security Council, concludes that covert actions carry such tremendous risks that the bureaucracy for covert operations itself, whether for covert action or for espionage, should be eliminated.

At the present time the CIA and other executive agencies provide intelligence information in such a way as to make it useful to special interest groups — as when the CIA invited 150 members of the American Institute of Aeronautics and Astronautics to a briefing. This body, which included foreign and domestic aircraft manufacturers, was briefed on Soviet space technology and given estimates that Israel has between 10 and 20 nuclear weapons "available for use." The *New York Times* suggested editorially that the CIA's statement about Israel may have been intended to encourage proposed arms shipments to Egypt at the time of Congressional and public opposition.

The executive branch also gives classified briefings to members of Congress with the stipulation that the Congress cannot use the information. Senator Dick Clark (D., Iowa) said after a briefing for the Senate Foreign Relations Committee that he could not publicize the information because "if I were to tell you that the United States was involved in covert activities in Angola, I could be kicked out of the Senate" John H. F. Shattuck, National staff counsel of ACLU, pointed out to a Congressional committee that "by restricting the flow of classified information to the Congress, there is no question that the executive can manipulate congressional decision-making processes" and thus render Congress impotent in a dispute between it and the executive.

Senator Stuart Symington, who served on both the Armed Forces and Foreign Relations Committees, illustrated the way executive denial of information to the public is used to manipulate Congressional decisions. From 1964 to 1969, the President was conducting a secret war in Laos. Symington did not know until the fall of 1969 that U.S. pilots based in Thailand were "bombing targets and napalming natives" in Laos. In an article in the *New York Times Magazine,* he reported that the Administration was secretly escalating the fighting in Laos while publicly announcing de-escalation of the war in Vietnam. The Administration misled the American people "as to the overall role of the United States in Southeast Asia, whereas the enemy—fully aware of the stepped-up United States bombing—received quite a different impression with respect to the actual intentions of our Government." When Congress finally was given some information about the secret war, it voted 73-17 an amendment prohibiting the sending of ground combat troops into Laos, but felt powerless to stop the war itself.

If the United States is to be an open society and if government is the servant rather than the master of the people, then the public, and not just Congress, has the right to know. If the people do not know what their government is doing, they cannot cast informed votes on election day. The whole structure of representative government and the principle of the consent of the governed are at stake if the government conducts covert operations which are designed to keep the American people from knowing and reacting. Congress cannot carry out its constitutional role in debating and formulating foreign and military policy or determining appropriations if the executive branch is permitted to keep secret matters in these fields.

When the CIA and other agencies of governments engage in covert operations there are also vast economic implications. These range from money and gifts used to corrupt individuals to illegal assistance of multinational corporations. The House Intelligence committee not only reported CIA secret purchases of "hundreds of refrigerators, televisions, cameras and watches . . . each year" but also "a variety of home furnishings" which suggest official corruption. It reported secret procurement of "custom-built armored limousines" and an "electronic intelligence network" for a ruthless dictator overseas. A major result of covert arrangements for intelligence gatherings is that multi-national and other corporations that help the CIA and other intelligence agencies receive favors in return. An example of this was revealed in an investigative report of Howard Hughes's companies in the *Philadelphia Inquirer* by

Donald L. Barlett and James B. Steele which stated: "Scores of employees from more than a half-dozen different agencies of the federal government—the Federal Bureau of Investigation to the Defense Department—move effortlessly from the government payroll to the Hughes payroll."

The people have a right to know who profits from CIA, FBI and military intelligence purchases. They have a right to know whether their taxes are used to deny civil liberties at home and abroad. They have a right to know if their taxes are financing multi-national corporations. At present they cannot know. The House Intelligence Committee reports that "there is no explanation from the FBI on the reasons for millions of dollars of 'confidential purchases.'" The committee also revealed that "our government auditors, the General Accounting Office, have been denied access to secret intelligence budgets for more than a decade."

Ironically, the Congressional and executive investigations have thus far strengthened rather than impeded the CIA in its covert activities. The President promised a sweeping reform of the intelligence community but moved instead to tighten the secrecy surrounding its activities, proposing a criminal penalty for any past or present government employee who discloses "information relating to intelligence sources and methods." The Congressional Committees merely want to oversee covert operations more thoroughly, not to abolish them.

What is needed is an end to covert action and a statute making it a crime for intelligence officials or other senior policy makers willfully to deceive Congress or the public regarding activities which violate the law.

XXI

Christian Worship of Violence

(St. Luke's Journal of Theology, September, 1981)

Any discussion of national security today must begin with a look at the nature of nuclear war. In February, 1980, the Harvard and Tufts Universities' medical schools sponsored a two-day symposium on the medical consequences of nuclear weapons. A large, heavily-scientific audience listened to Dean Hiatt of the Harvard School of Public Health describe the effects of a single nuclear weapon on the Boston area. The weapon was a thousand times as powerful as the Hiroshima bomb but by no means the largest now in world arsenals. Anthony Lewis wrote in the *Kansas City Times* (February 15, 1980):

"That weapon would destroy everything within four miles. The bomb crater itself would be a half a mile in diameter and several hundred feet deep. Beyond the four-mile radius of total destruction, a pressure wave, followed by winds of over 1,000 miles an hour, would build an enormous fire storm. Forty miles away, people looking in the direction of the explosion would be blinded by retinal burns." (It would be virtually certain that anyone who heard such an explosion or experienced the light would turn almost instinctively to look at it.)

"Of the 3 million people living in the Boston metropolitan area, 2.2 million would be killed at once by the blast or fire storm. Of the survivors, Hiatt said, many 'are badly burned, blinded and otherwise seriously wounded. Many are disoriented. These are the short term effects; the problem of radiation sickness will grow.'

"Most of Boston's great hospitals would have been destroyed. Of the 6,560 doctors in the area, almost 5,000 would be dead and only 900 in physical condition to work. If doctors spent an average of 15 minutes with each injured person and worked 16 hours a day, it would take about three weeks for each casualty to be seen once.

"'One of the most serious post-attack public health problems,' Hiatt said, 'is disposal of the dead. The presence of more than 2.2 million bodies will pose a continuing and serious hazard to the health of the survivors.'"

In the 1970's, Presidential Review Memorandum No. 10, which dealt with military strategy, indicated that in a nuclear war between the United States and the Soviet Union the U.S. would suffer 140 million casualties and the Russians 113 million with about 75% of their respective economies devastated. That Memorandum came to the conclusion that "neither side could conceivably be described as a winner."

Nevertheless there are powerful forces in the U.S. that are planning for nuclear war. James Schlesinger, former Secretary of Defense, spoke for this group immediately after the United States was defeated in Vietnam when he said that in the future it would "be necessary to go for the heart of the opponent's power; destroy his military forces rather than simply being involved endlessly in ancillary military operations."

Schlesinger also announced a shift in U.S. military strategy away from missiles aimed only at Russian cities so as to deter a Soviet attack — to a counter force strategy aimed at destroying Soviet missile silos and missile-firing submarines. On the surface this seemed like a more humane approach to war in that we would aim at weapons rather than at population centers. Actually this new counter-force strategy, which President Carter made official in Presidential Directive 59, presupposes a surprise attack or first-strike against the Soviet Union, because if they get their missiles launched first American missiles would be striking only empty missile silos.

The United States now has more than 30,000 nuclear weapons stockpiled, almost 10,000 of which are strategic weapons capable of destroying cities of 100,000 or more people when fired from the U.S. or from a submarine. These are equal in explosive power to 76,363 Hiroshima bombs. Our entire stockpile equals the explosive power of 615,385 Hiroshima bombs.

If the Pentagon were to use its arsenal of nuclear weapons or even a fraction of them against the Soviet Union, and if the weapons of that country were to be destroyed so that there was no retaliation, millions upon millions of Americans would nevertheless be destroyed by the radioactivity from our own weapons which the air currents would carry to us.

Philip Handler, President of the National Academy of Science, wrote that such a war would deplete the protective layer of ozone in the stratosphere and that this would result in such intense ultra-violet irradiation of the earth's surface as to cause crop failure by direct damage to plants and by major alterations to climate. He added, "No nation can deliver what is intended as a massive pre-emptive strike without automatic, catastrophic natural damage to itself."

The first thing we can say about nuclear war is that it is impossible to eliminate our enemies without risking our own extinction. In other words, war destroys those it was designed to defend as well as those it was intended to destroy. So, for the first time in human history, Jesus' words become literally true: "Those who take the sword will perish by the sword." Even in the nuclear age most people are unprepared to follow Jesus' advice to put away their weapons. Bertrand Russell concluded that "Human beings are more eager to kill their enemies than to stay alive themselves."

The second thing we can say about nuclear war is that it reveals God's will about organized violence. Just as the nature of an oak tree is more evident in its full development than it is in the acorn, so the destructiveness of nuclear war reveals more fully God's indictment of armed force than was evident in the use of swords and spears. Yet centuries ago the Hebrew prophets proclaimed to their nation that God willed peace. Both Micah and Isaiah looked forward to the day when people would beat their swords into plowshares and their spears into pruning hooks.

The third thing we can say about war is that through nuclear weapons God is confronting the human race with a life-and-death decision. In effect, God is saying, "You humans have been unwilling voluntarily to form a world-wide human community but have organized yourselves into armed nations. Now you have a choice between a disarmed world community or nuclear destruction." If the instinct of race preservation is still present in the human species, God is in effect coercing us through the fact of nuclear weapons to abolish war and achieve reconciliation with our enemies.

Although God wills peace and the facts of nuclear war indicate that disarmament is a necessity, there are at least three things which stand in the way of disarmament.

The first is a popular belief that the manufacture and stockpiling of weapons is actually the best way to prevent war. This theory of deterrence is based on the assumption that if each nation is able to destroy its adversary neither side will dare to attack. Nuclear deterrence therefore means that the entire civilian population of another nation is treated as a hostage for the conduct of its armed forces. This is a direct reversal of the Golden Rule. Instead of doing unto others as we would want them to do unto us, deterrence means: "Be prepared to do unto others what we don't want them to do unto us — and they won't do it." This theory of deterrence is incredibly stupid and brutal. Instead of trying to win people in other nations by policies that would encourage them not to seek our destruction, we tell them that their total population is targeted for destruction in the event of war. Even the opponents of regimes we dislike become our enemies rather than our friends.

Deterrence does not prevent war. The Nairobi Conference of the World Council of Churches reminded us that since World War II more than a hundred wars have been fought, causing the deaths of more than 1 million people in about sixty countries.

The failure of deterrence is most clearly illustràted by President Kennedy's decision, during the Cuban Missile Crisis, to engage in nuclear war against the Soviet Union. Robert Kennedy told the story in his book, *Thirteen Days: A Memoir of the Cuban Missile Crisis,* which first appeared under the subtitle, *The Story About How The World Almost Ended.* On his first page, President Kennedy's brother and closest adviser called the crisis "a confrontation between the two giant atomic nations, the U.S. and the U.S.S.R., which brought the world to the abyss of nuclear destruction and the end of mankind."

The crisis arose first because Soviet missiles were put in Cuba, as American missiles had been put in Turkey. The final crisis arose when the U.S. rejected the offer of the Soviet Union to settle the matter peacefully by simultaneous removal of both sets of missiles. The U.S. sent an ultimatum to the Soviets. Robert Kennedy took that ultimatum to the Soviet Ambassador, and this is his report of what was said: "We [the U.S.] had to have a commitment by tomorrow that these bases would be removed. He should understand that if they did not remove those bases, we would remove them. He asked me what offer the U.S. was making. He raised the question of our removing our missiles from Turkey. I said there could be no *quid pro quo* or any arrangement. I returned to the White House. The President was not optimistic, nor was I. He ordered twenty-four troup carrier squadrons of Air Force Reserve to active duty. They would be necessary for invasion. He had not abandoned hope, but what hope there was now rested with Khruschev's revising his course within the next four hours. It was a hope, not an expectation. The expectation was a military confrontation by Tuesday and possibly tomorrow."

Robert Kennedy further reported what the President expected to result from this war. "The thought that disturbed him the most, and that made the prospect of war much more fearful than it would otherwise have been, was the specter of the death of the children of this country and all the world — the young people who had no role, who had no say, who knew nothing even of the confrontation, but whose lives would be snuffed out like everyone else's."

"Thus it was judged better to end the human world," wrote Prof. John Somerville, "than to grant equal rights to the Soviets, and the only reason it didn't end then was that the Soviets unexpectedly obeyed the ultimatum."

150

The lesson to be learned from this incident is that the United States was not deterred by the danger of a Soviet nuclear retaliation. It was not even deterred by the thought of total human destruction.

The second thing that stands in the way of disarmament is the military-industrial complex and the military-minded leaders of government, labor, and industry. They want arms control rather than disarmament. Arms control is an attempt to avoid disarmament by setting limits on armaments that will strengthen your own nation at the expense of another. Gerard C. Smith, who was chief of the U.S. delegation at the Strategic Arms Limitation Talks, known as SALT, from 1969-1972 said: "In effect we were trying to get an arrangement that would limit Soviet modernization programs but not our own. . . . We were trying to fix constraints on Soviet programs that would not affect American programs." An illustration of arms control is the Vladivostok agreements which limited each side to a total of 2,400 long range missiles and bombers. Of that number, 1,320 could be MIRV warheads. Since neither side had that many missiles, this encouraged the expansion rather than the reduction of arms.

The third thing that stands in the way of disarmament is Christian worship of violence. If we define God as that which is ultimately decisive in world affairs, then the God of most people is violence. It is variously stated in such ideas as "power grows out of the barrel of a gun;" or "the only language those people will understand is force;" or "the way to prevent war is by the threat of certain destruction;" or "the outcome of human history will be determined by the nations with superior armed force." Such commitment to armed violence is idolatry and can only keep us from the living God and the security that comes from opening our minds to other methods of dealing with rival nations.

Most Americans have been concerned about the risks of disarmament rather than the risks of nuclear weapons and war. They assume that anything justifies the destruction of our enemies including mass murder in the hundreds of millions, poisoning the human genes and the earth itself.

We must recognize that in the nuclear age the war system is the enemy, and the people of other nations, like ourselves, have nothing to gain by its continuance. If a nation were completely disarmed and, therefore, no threat to any nuclear power, there would be no reason for that nation to want to destroy it. But if nuclear war came to any armed nation, it would be destroyed regardless of the size or effectiveness of its armed forces.

Armaments can no longer defend the United States. The idea of preventing an attack on our country is a concept of the days before the development of intercontinental missiles. It is not possible for any government to stop or to intercept missiles as used to be the case when our fleet or submarines could intercept and destroy a naval invasion force.

We view the Russians as our enemies not because they are communists but because they have armaments capable of conquering and destroying other nations. We would not fear a completely disarmed Soviet Union as they would not fear a disarmed United States.

It is human nature for us to want to blame our opponents for the failure to achieve disarmament. We should remember that in 1955, when the U.S., the British and the French proposed a genuine disarmament program which would have disarmed all nations down to internal police forces, the Soviet Union accepted it in principle. We were not serious in our proposal. Our negotiator was called back to the United States and the plan was withdrawn. The U.S. in its entire history has never signed a disarmament treaty that did not permit us to increase our armaments. There have been six thousand meetings in the last thirty years to discuss nuclear disarmament and not one bomb has been destroyed.

We must ask ourselves seriously whether we Christians can support a system that is organized for and plans to destroy millions of persons in other nations who are also children of God. What value is our religious commitment or the ecumenical church if we can destroy our fellow Christians and Jews, and our brothers and sisters in other countries? We must begin to call upon Russians and Poles and Czechs and Germans as well as Americans to demand disarmament of their own countries.

Now it is possible that some of you may not be moved to act for disarmament because you do not feel the same urgency I feel. If you can imagine your city and the entire area hit by nuclear weapons with two-thirds of the people killed instantly while you die gradually over a two week period and watch your children or grandchildren die — then you would wish that in the preceding three or four or ten years you had done everything you could to have made war impossible.

The problem is not only our failure to imagine the future but our unwillingness to commit ourselves to any risk. It is commonplace to talk about the threat and undesirability of nuclear war. Every group of Christians, including the World Council of Churches, the Pope, the National Council of Churches have called on governments to come to some agreement on the abolition of nuclear weapons. But these appeals have had no effect.

Martin Buber, the Jewish philosopher, commenting on this, said that "these appeals failed because the people making them were not committed. They only said what other people ought to do — those in governments. . . . They never stated what the authors of those appeals would do themselves, nor to what they committed themselves."

Many years ago, while I was a student in law school, I made a commitment at a National Conference of Methodist Youth. That group of young people had a motto which went like this: "Henceforth, I shall live as if the Kingdom of God were already here. Therefore, if in the Kingdom there is no racial discrimination, for me there shall be none. And if in the Kingdom there is no warfare, for me there shall be none." This is another way of saying that all other loyalties are relativized. My primary loyalty is not to the white race but to humanity. My primary loyalty is not to the nation-state but to God's people everywhere.

The goal of God is to bring humans into the Kingdom of God. This necessarily involves a break with other loyalties such as racism and nationalism.

If we want disarmament we have got to repent of our commitment to the existing order and begin to change. Repentance means this. I have no control over the leaders of the Soviet Union or of any other nation. The only person over whom I have any control is myself. Therefore, if I want to change the world I must start at the point where I have some control, my own self, my own church, my own college, my own community, and my own nation. It is pointless to ask other nations to do the right thing first. According to Hebrew-Christian praxis the initiative must always be ours.

XXII

The Holy War Mentality

(*Fellowship*, April/May, 1981)

European, Asian, and North American nations are sitting on a precarious peace while wars in the Middle East, Africa and Central America nibble at their edges. Meanwhile, the United States and the Soviet Union are involved in an arms race, with the Soviet goal that of nuclear parity while the U.S. seeks to maintain and expand its supremacy.

The rivalry between the U.S. and the U.S.S.R. is not the primary problem in international relations. It is, however, the only credible excuse for expanding the U.S. military budget and the U.S. armed forces. The Soviet Union has lost ground in recent years, with such former allies as Somalia, Egypt, and China having established a working relationship with the U.S. It is bogged down in Afghanistan by guerrilla war and threatened by unrest in Poland. The U.S.S.R. maintains 650,000 troops at the end of a long supply line on the Chinese border and continues to supply Cuba, its one ally in the western hemisphere, with about $3 million of aid each day. It has few reliable allies, is surrounded on all sides by hostile nations, and is targeted by the nuclear missiles of at least four nations.

The U.S. on the other hand, is not threatened by any neighbor and is not likely to be attacked by the Soviet Union. The concern of the American foreign policy establishment is chiefly to protect the American empire, including U.S. business investments around the world. Stated negatively, this means preventing third-world nations, such as El Salvador, from establishing anti-imperialist or anti-U.S. regimes. The arena for Soviet-American rivalry is in the third world but the primary problem for the American empire is not Soviet penetration of those nations; it is the growing opposition to oppressive regimes within nations that have had long-term U.S. military or economic support.

If the Soviet Union is the excuse, and control of the third world is the reason for the arms race, the primary beneficiary is the military-industrial complex. The arms race is crucial to the income security or profits of many corporations. Apparently, little can be done politically now to prevent the increase in the military budget at the expense of the social welfare and other budgets that do not aid big business. Social welfare budgets are a threat to the military-industrial complex because they compete with the military for appropriations and because the bureaucracies of Health, Education, Welfare, Housing and Urban Development and other agencies share in the direction of government. Together with their constituencies, they are a modest counter lobby to expanding military interests.

Although the U.S. is primarily concerned with maintaining and expanding its economic and military influence around the world, the danger of nuclear war flows from the fact of American and Soviet missiles and the possibility that wars between U.S. and Soviet allies might trigger a larger war.

The danger of a confrontation with the Soviet Union is increased by the U.S. naval and military presence in the Middle East, which occurred as a result of the Iranian revolution and the Soviet intervention in Afghanistan. With NATO on the European flank of the Soviets and Chinese troops on the Asian flank, the U.S. force in the Middle East can be seen as an effort to close the gap of containment.

The U.S. deployment force there has at least three other purposes. The first is to try to hold the lid on any explosive situation that might invite Soviet assistance. "Every single regime in the Middle East, without exception, is in danger of upheaval," according to Dr. Charles Malik of Lebanon, who was once the President of the U.N. General Assembly. The second reason is to protect American oil interests. The third is to rebuild American influence which was lost when the Iranian revolution eliminated Iran as the chief U.S. deputy in the region.

Egypt has now replaced Iran in that role. The Carter Camp David talks and the Egyptian-Israeli peace have paid off for the U.S., and for Egypt as well. The U.S. has given Egypt more than $53 billion in economic aid. On a per capita basis, the Egyptians are getting more American aid in real dollars than West Europeans received after World War II. Egyptian officers, civilian instructors and maintenance specialists have been training in the U.S. Egypt has become the key to American ability to exert influence in Africa and the Persian Gulf oil nations.

In Latin America, El Salvador has become the symbol of American determination to stop and reverse any efforts at national liberation in this hemisphere. Socialist mediation of the conflict or some other development may prevent the U.S. intervening as it did in the Dominican Republic a few years back, but that decision will not be out of any deference to a principled objection to interference in the affairs of other nations.

The Chief Cause of Inflation

Given the U.S. rearmament program and military efforts to shore up the American empire in Latin America and the Middle East, disarmament is a long-term goal with little hope of immediate implementation. But there are short-term goals which, if achieved, would increase the chance of eventual nuclear disarmament. These include prevention of military inervention in Central America, stopping the MX missile program, and keeping out of war in the Middle East. Billions of dollars would be saved.

The enormous flow of dollars required by the U.S. emphasis on global military supremacy is not having the intended effect. The economic strength of a nation has always been more of a key to power than military might. By steadily sapping this nation's economic strength, military spending is actually weakening the U.S. effort to maintain global hegemony. It is the chief cause of debilitating inflation and unemployment. Officers, soldiers, workers and management in the military-industrial complex are the conduit for billions of dollars of purchasing power that flow into the civilian economy. But the armed forces and war industry produce nothing for civilians to purchase. That excess purchasing power forces up prices. Waste is encouraged when the Pentagon pays actual cost plus ten percent profit, because there is an incentive to expand rather than hold down the cost. The cost-plus program only adds to inflation.

Military industry uses more highly skilled labor and fewer workers than many civilian employers. Economizing on civilian projects in order to permit increased military spending leads to increased unemployment. The high cost of petroleum products also drives up costs for everyone.

High interest rates increase the profits of banks, but when no one can affort to borrow money, housing deteriorates, small business fail, and industrial plants are unable to keep up with advancing technology. The chief function of high interest, inflation, and unemployment is to redistribute income from the lower to the upper economic classes. In effect, the rich segment of society is engaged in class warfare against the middle and lower income groups, and against the population as a whole, as environmental, agricultural, and industrial resources deteriorate.

No Real Shift to the Right

The political base for the Reagan administration and the military-industrial complex is not as large as the last election seems to indicate. The New Right and the "Moral Majority" are not symbolic of a popular shift to the right, nor has public opinion moved in their direction. Reagan's election by about twenty-seven percent of the electorate was the result of anti-Carter sentiment and the lack of a Democratic Party program for dealing with inflation, unemployment, and the arms race. Even the convergence of numerous single issue groups relating to sex, abortion, guns, school prayer, and other matters was not a decisive factor. The crucial factors in the election , according to all polls, were economic and international. This does not alter the fact that Congress, as well as the administration, is largely in the hands of right wing forces which will neglect the poor, civil liberties, and human rights.

On the domestic scene it is obvious that there is no independent labor movement to give leadership against the present trend. There is no viable left-of-center movement either intellectually or organizationally capable of leading the nation away from economic and military disaster. The contemporary political movements with mass support are environmental and feminist. Both are important but have no economic and international program. Some national leaders of the churches are concerned about peace and justice, but there is little activity at the crucial local level and not much in the theological schools. The churches have no clear conviction that war as such is incompatible with faith in God or with humanism or ecumenism. There is far more Christian preoccupation with the issue of abortion than with the danger of annihilation of the human race. Neither pacifism nor socialism is as much an issue today as each was in the twenties or thirties.

There is also an increasing lack of concern about public education evident in the cutting of school budgets to save taxes, in the proliferation of private schools for racial and religious reasons, and in the acceptance of segregated and deteriorating school neighborhoods. The use of the schools for national military purposes, such as recruiting, and the administration of armed forces vocational aptitude tests, is also a sign that the schools are being subordinated to values other than learning.

The Impending Draft

The draft can still be defeated, but not by generalized opposition to it. There is a virtual certainty of its eventual passage unless opposition is focussed at the following three points: First, it needs to focus on Congressional insistence that the armed forces must have at least sixty-five to seventy-five percent of its recruits who are high school graduates. When the high school dropout rate is fifty-five to sixty-five percent in some cities, the pool of high school graduates available for recruiting will be small. The Senators who proposed that recruits must be high school graduates know that such quotas cannot be filled without a draft. Secondly, the racist attitude in the statement that there are too many blacks in the Army needs to be questioned. This is not a concern for blacks but a fear among prejudiced whites that blacks won't fight well against the darker-skinned people of the third world. Thirdly, opposition must be mounted to any increase in the size of the armed forces. The armed forces exist chiefly for overseas activity that will defend the American empire. Opposition to war and imperialism requires that they be reduced rather than expanded.

The U.S. faces an unparalleled crisis that touches almost every aspect of American life. The moral nerve of social action has not been cut but there is no political or theological alternative to the present trend around which opponents of that trend are prepared to rally. In some respects, the crucial battle we face in America is theological. Instead of recognizing that the enemy is systemic and internal, there is a clear assumption on the part of most Americans that the U.S. leads the forces of good while the U.S.S.R. leads the forces of evil, and that the U.S. must remain ahead in its ability to meet the forces of evil on the battlefield. At the root of the refusal even to discuss disarmament with the Soviet Union is a distrust of negotiations or compromise with the devil.

This tragic, holy war mentality is nourished by the military-industrial complex and is almost totally ignored by the churches. Given the almost certain result of nuclear holocaust in the event of war, we humans seem to be more concerned with killing our enemies, as Bertrand Russell concluded a few years back, than with staying alive ourselves.

XXIII

Peace Conversion

(Fellowship, April/May, 1978)

Many Americans oppose reduction in armaments in the mistaken belief that the U.S. economy could not survive without the tremendous sums that continually pour into industry through the military budget. To all practical purposes, the American people accept without analysis the myth that the economy is dependent upon this hugh military outlay. The myth has been encouraged by Marxists, who insist that capitalism cannot survive without a war economy. It has also been fostered by those with a vested interest in the military-industrial complex.

Even so, a large number of Americans wanted to reduce military spending following the Vietnam War. In the fall of 1974, the Gallup Poll reported that forty-four percent of those interviewed believed that the United States was spending too much for military purposes. Last spring, Rep. Parren Mitchell (D-Md.) led a campaign in Congress to transfer billions of dollars from the 1978 military budget to programs that would meet human needs. While that move was unsuccessful, it is expected to be the forerunner of additional efforts at arms reduction. (Another transfer amendment has been put before Congress this year.) Such legislation is responsive not only to the political pressure for meeting the survival needs of millions of poor Americans but to the growing body of evidence that a high level of military spending creates unemployment.

An analysis made by a group of economists headed by Dr. John Henderson, former Director of Graduate Studies in the Michigan State Economics Department, indicates that for the years 1968-1972 the net annual job loss in the United States at a time when the military budget averaged about $80 billion was about 840,000 jobs. They discovered that for each billion dollars spent by the government only 55,000 civilian defense jobs are created, whereas the same amount spent on sewer construction or public housing would create 76,000 jobs or would employ

100,000 teachers or 151,000 persons in the job corps. State and local government expenditures nationwide generate about 100,000 jobs for every billion dollars spent.

The reason for this difference in jobs generated by government spending, according to Ruth Sivard, an economist formerly employed by the Arms Control and Disarmament Agency, is this: "Defense production tends to require more highly skilled people but to employ fewer people per unit of output than civilian industry."

Dr. Henderson and his team of economists also discovered that when spending on the military went up, expenditures on civilian jobs went down by certain definite percentages in such categories as durable goods, non-durable goods, state and local government expenditures, residential and non-residential construction, services, and exports. New York state lost 426,000 jobs; Michigan, Illinois and Ohio together lost 492,000. The negative impact of Pentagon spending upon the industrial base of the fifty states far outweighed the jobs they gained through military contracts and bases. The only exceptions to this were Georgia, Texas and California, which together gained 285,000 jobs.

It is not simply that a civilian economy creates jobs, but that military-industrial firms tend to have a lower ratio of profits to sales as compared to civilian manufacturing firms. Dr. John J. Kennedy of Ohio State University reported that in 1959 profit as a percentage of sales for defense firms was 2.6 percent, compared with 6.4 percent for non-defense firms. Murray L. Weidenbaum of Washington University reported profits on sales by defense firms (1962-1965) as 2.6 percent and for a sample of average civilian industrial firms as 4.6 percent.

If we examine the economy as a whole compared to our two chief foreign competitors, we discover that more military activity does not mean greater output or an improved capitalism. In 1968, the military spending of the U.S. was 9.2 percent of the gross national product as compared to West Germany's 3.9 percent and Japan's 0.8 percent. However, the growth rate in output per employee was 9.5 percent for Japan, 4.6 percent for West Germany, and only 2.6 percent for the U.S. during the years 1960-69.

There are various ways of effecting savings in the military budget. One is to eliminate the tremendous waste. Seymour Melman of Columbia University reports that in 1969, at the peak of the Vietnam War, the military had 18,277 Army colonels and Navy captains in an armed force of 3.5 million. But in 1945, when there were 12 million in the armed forces, there were only 14,898 colonels and (naval) captains on duty. By December of 1969, there was one officer or non-commissioned officer to supervise every two enlisted men. Melmen's report showed the armed forces to be top-heavy with expensive officers. It also revealed how money allocated for weapons is wasted. "When the U.S. Government Accounting Office did an audit of the operations of major Lockheed factories working on the C-5 airplane," he wrote, "they found that about 8.6 percent of the production's assembly employees were idle and that the whereabouts of a further 6.2 percent could not be determined from co-workers or supervisors."

Savings in the range of $15 billion could be achieved by ending wasteful practices, by using competitive bidding, and by cancelling production of unnecessary weapons.

A second way of reducing military spending is through a changed foreign policy. All the armed forces designed to achieve or maintain U.S. control over other countries, or to launch a Vietnam-type intervention, could be terminated. This would include cutting out more than 30,000 troops in South Korea, 30,000 more from Okinawa, Taiwan, and the Philippines, and 30,000 held in the U.S. for Asian intervention. It would include ending CIA covert intervention abroad, as well as military aid and sale of arms to dictatorships. It would end nuclear weapons production and testing. In addition, most of the strategic nuclear forces could be eliminated; they represent what some military men term "unnecessary overkill." Seymour Melman estimated a few years ago that if such cutbacks were made on a world-wide basis, the U.S. total security cost would be no more than $29 billion. This, he said, would release more than sixty to seventy billion dollars of public money for productive uses.

Leonard A. Lecht of the National Planning Association has estimated that if $20 billion were cut from the defense budget, with half going into social programs and half staying in private coffers through tax reduction, new job openings would exceed by 425,000 those lost through military cutbacks. The new jobs would require different skills. There would be fewer engineers and machine operators and more service personnel, craftsmen, and laborers.

Richard Barnett has proposed a National Conversion Commission to make an inventory of national needs, such as medical schools, public schools, and programs for cleaning the nation's rivers and converting to solar, wind and hydraulic energy. He also proposed that every community with substantial military spending should "be required to prepare a local reconversion plan as a condition of receiving further federal grants of any kind."

A national effort backed by careful planning would undoubtedly be necessary if the United States were to disarm or drastically to reduce military spending. But local communities can engage in local conversion from a military to a civilian economy without national planning. The evidence that it can be done is in Salina, Kansas, a city of 39,000 people.

Salina was given six months' notice when the Department of Defense closed Schilling Air Force base in 1965. At first glance, it seemed to threaten economic disaster; some 5,000 military personnel were to be transferred elsewhere. The base was the area's major employer, with an annual payroll of $22 million. It maintained a population of at least 13,000, when civilian employees and military families were included. Business firms related to the base closed overnight, and retail sales dropped $7 million in a year. Then the city began to take advantage of its adversity or, as someone put it, "when life gives you lemons make lemonade." The city built the air base into an 1,800-acre municipal airport, able to handle more than 1,000 operations a year. It is served by seven daily passenger flights and is a frequent stop for business people on cross-country jet flights. The main runway is used by two major airlines for pilot training in 747 and 707 aircraft.

The city developed the former air base area into an industrial park where seventy business firms now employ 3,000 workers. The two largest employers are Tony's Pizza with 1,200 employees and Beech Aircraft with 800. They occupy large buildings from the old base, which have been adapted to civilian use. There are houseware and farm machinery manufacturers in the park, as well. The Kansas Highway patrol trains new troopers where military crews were once on alert duty. A chinchilla farm thrives where nuclear weapons once were stored. Where sentry dogs were caged, there is now a civilian dog kennel.

As soon as the Pentagon releases the 735-unit base housing complex, the city plans to make it into a retirement home and low-income housing. The state helped by moving the Kansas Vocational Rehabilitation Center into the 75-bed base hospital, while the Kansas Technological Institute took over educational buildings on the base for its three hundred students.

John Scanlan, who was base commander when Schilling closed and who is now executive vice-president of the airport authority, claims the city's success stems from having "bought the idea it was going to close without a scrap." The executive vice-president of the Salina area Chamber of Commerce said last year: "The community is better off today than it was in 1964. We're more diversified. It's been healthy."

It is time to recognize that the strength of local communities, as well as the nation, resides in civilian production that meets human needs. Military production and bases create buying power but do not produce goods that can be bought in the market. Military business not only tends to induce inflation, but also to create unemployment. Huge military budgets are harmful to the economy and therefore damaging to the economic base on which American security ultimately depends.

XXIV

U.S. Double Standard Nicaragua's Chief Foe

(National Catholic Reporter, June 3, 1983)

The picture of Nicaragua painted by President Reagan is far from reality in almost every respect. That was the startling conclusion of five representatives of religious and peace organizations who recently returned from a fact-finding mission to Nicaragua and Honduras.

As a member of that group, I talked freely with people in various parts of the country: university professors, farmers, soldiers in the border battle area, missionaries, and many others. It is certainly the most open society in Latin America and shows a greater respect for the poor than any of the many countries I have visited during the past 20 years.

Contrary to White House assertions, it is not a Communist society. The small Communist party is not represented on the three-man junta or the nine-member directorate which named the junta in 1979. One of the three junta, Rafael Cordova Rivas, is a member of the Conservative party of Nicaragua. The other two are Sandinistas, who consider themselves the vanguard of the revolution rather than a political party. The other parties include the Christian Democrats, the Liberal party, the Social Democrats, and the Socialist party.

Each political party, depending on its size, has one or more representatives in the *Consela de Estado* of 51 people. This state council also includes representatives of other interest groups such as the Catholic clergy, Protestants, landowners, women, professional, farmers, and workers groups. These people are elected by their organizations. The organizations themselves discuss their problems and their desires. Organized teachers, for example, play an important role in education decisions. Base groups in every working center and school discuss and pass their ideas on to the national organization. In this way there is a two-way communication with the state council, which functions like a congress. Nicaragua has already had municipal and county elections and in 1985 plans nation-wide elections.

An official in the U.S. embassy in Honduras told us that Nicaragua is a Communist state but conceded under questioning that there is a difference between Communism and Marxism. He finally asserted that Nicaragua is a Marxist state. However, the Sandinistas have produced a mixed economy rather than one owned and operated by a party or state. Twenty percent of the land is state owned; 80 percent is owned privately or by cooperatives. Twenty-five percent of industry is state owned; 75 percent is private. The most obvious illustration of Marxism is the nationalization of the banks. Yet the White House does not speak of Mexico as Marxist although both the oil industry and the banks have been nationalized.

There is no military conscription in Nicaragua in spite of the CIA-led war on the northern border. Both the regular armed force and the militia are staffed by volunteer men and women imbued with the desire to keep their country free from the control of the U.S. and Anastasio Somoza's National Guard mobilized on the border. No one knows how many pacifists there are because there is no tradition of objection to war. However, perhaps as many as 15 percent of the people oppose the revolution and therefore could not be expected to join the militia. The other evidences of a free society include the right to join labor unions and bargain collectively, access to government leaders, and free speech.

The chief illustration of a restriction on freedom is censorship. The director of *La Prensa* told us he must submit newspaper copy to a government office which sometimes excises whole columns. The government, however, claims that beginning with the CIA-sponsored border warfare, it became necessary to censor *La Prensa* because it was manipulated by the CIA according to the pattern the CIA used in papers in Chile and Jamaica to topple governments there.

La Prensa continues to have freedom to publish, and its staff enjoy complete freedom in Nicaragua. Such freedom for journalists does not exist in El Salvador or Guatemala, Chile or Haiti, yet the Reagan administration does not make a point of criticizing these governments as it does Nicaragua.

Although it is important to expose Reagan's double standard in judging press freedom in Latin America, it is essential that we engage in criticism where the government of Nicaragua falls short of its professed democratic principles. Full freedom for *La Prensa* to publish hostile comments or factually incorrect stories should be guaranteed. Exposure in other papers of factually incorrect data would deal with the problem.

Another illustration of censorship came from Father Bismarck Carballo, the press director and representative of Archbishop Miguel Obando y Bravo of Managua. He told us there was censorship of the Roman Catholic-owned radio station, that it "is not allowed to carry news programs" or "present mass or celebrations of the word, live. During Somoza we had mass over TV and radio."

Adrien Zoller, a Swiss leader of Pax Christi who joined us for the interview, responded: "We have heard masses on the radio since 1981, when you said there were none. Isn't it true that the Sandistas said, each Sunday there had to be a different bishop giving mass over the radio and the archbishop refused to do this?"

There is obviously a church-state confrontation between the archbishop and the Sandinista government. We learned that Obando y Bravo went to Washington on the invitation of Constantin Menge, hemisphere director of CIA for Latin America, to receive an award from the Institute of Religion and Democracy.

On another occasion, Carballo visited the U.S. I asked, "Who invited you to visit the United States in August, 1982?" He said, "It was a program of foreign visitors. It was not the church." Under further questioning he admitted "the invitation came from the U.S. embassy" and "my expenses were paid."

The Sandinista leaders announced two years ago total respect for religion and asked respect for all Christian groups. Nevertheless some Sandinistas had difficulty in understanding Jehovah's Witnesses, Seventh Day Adventists and Mormons, whose property they confiscated. Dr. Parajon, a Harvard-trained physician who works with the Evangelical Committee for Aid and Development (CEPAD), made up of 37 denominations, told us there are approximately 80 denominations in Nicaragua. He said CEPAD, which meets at least once a month with representatives of the junta and directorate, talked to these government leaders about the confiscated property, and it was given back.

We heard again and again that all of the Protestant groups as well as the priests and nuns who work with the people acknowledge that there is religious liberty previously unknown in Nicaragua under Somoza. Under Somoza the government used to finance the Catholic church, but not now. However, Obando was offered the same amount of money he was getting from Somoza, but he refused. Carballo said "the Catholic school system has been maintained. Forty percent of schools are Catholic, but because of financial difficulties, many have passed into the hands of the state." He said "the government authorized Catholic education in the schools, but it has to be after school hours."

Curriculum
Vitae

JOHN M. SWOMLEY, JR.
9203 Rocky Point Drive
Kansas City, MO 64152
January, 1985

EDUCATION
University of Colorado, Ph.D. (Political Science), 1958.
Boston University, S.T.B., 1940; M.A., 1939.
Dickinson College, B.A., 1936.
John Harris High School, Harrisburg, Pennsylvania, 1932.

APPOINTMENTS
Professor Emeritus, Saint Paul School of Theology, July, 1984.
Professor, Christian Social Ethics and Philosophy of Religion, 1965-1984.
Visiting Lecturer, United Theological College, Salisbury, Rhodesia, 1977.
Visiting Professor of Social Ethics, Union Theological Seminary, Manila, P.I., 1973.
Professor Visitante de Etica Sociale, Facultad Evangelica de Teologia, Buenos Aires, Argentina, 1969.
Associate Professor, Christian Social Ethics and Philosophy of Religion, Saint Paul School of Theology, 1960-1964.
Executive Secretary, Fellowship of Reconciliation, 1953-1960.
Associate Executive Secretary, Fellowship of Reconciliation, 1944-1953.
On leave to direct National Campaign Against University Military Training, Washington, D.C., 1945-1952.
National Youth Secretary, Fellowship of Reconciliation, 1940-1943.

APPOINTMENTS PART-TIME
Interim Minister, United Church of Christ, Higginsville, Missouri 1974-1975.
Consultant on Ethics and Values, Chancellor's Task Force for the California State University System, 1973-1974.
Consultant, Institute for Non-Violence, London, England, 1966.
New England Secretary, Fellowship of Reconciliation, 1939-1940.
Youth Worker, Boston, MA., Y.M.C.A., 1938.
State Senate of Pennsylvania, 1932-1936.

OFFICES
President Methodist Peace Fellowship, 1965-.
Chairperson, Church-State Committee of American Civil Liberties Union, 1979-.
Member, National Board, American Civil Liberties Union, 1970-.
Member, Executive Committee, American Civil Liberties, Union, 1980-.
Member, Consultative Council, National Interreligious Service Board for Conscientious Objectors, 1982-.
Member, Board, Martin Luther King Urban Center, Kansas City, Kansas 1984-.
Member, Advisory Council, A. J. Muste Memorial Institute, 1982-.
Member, Board, Americans for Religious Liberty, 1983-.
Member, Board, Kansas City Interfaith Peace Alliance, 1981-.
Member, Executive Committee and Board Americans United, 1981-1983.

Member, National Council and Executive Committee, Fellowship of Reconciliation, 1970-1981.

President, American Civil Liberties Union of Western Missouri and Greater Kansas City, 1969-1973.

Member, Board of Directors, American Society of Christian Social Ethics, 1964-1969.

Member, General Board of Christian Social Concerns, United Methodist Church, 1964-1972.

Member, Committee on Civil and Religious Liberty, National Council of Churches, 1962-1970; 1980-.

Vice President, National Council of Methodist Youth, 1938-1941.

MEMBERSHIP IN PROFESSIONAL ORGANIZATIONS

New York Conference of the Methodist Church, 1954-1969.

Kansas East Conference, the United Methodist Church, 1969-.

American Political Science Association.

American Society of Christian Social Ethics.

AWARDS AND HONORS

American Humanist Association, Humanist Pioneer Award for year 1985.

Fellowship of Reconciliation, Honorary National Vice President, 1982-.

Kansas City's World Citizen of the Year 1976 (Mayor's United Nations Day Committee).

Patrick Murphy Malin Award for Outstanding Service to the Cause of Civil Liberties in Western Missouri and Greater Kansas City, 1975.

Phi Beta Kappa, 1936.

Tau Kappa Alpha, Honorary Forensic Society, 1935.

Pennsylvania State Oratorical Contest, First Place, 1932.

PUBLICATIONS – BOOKS

The Military Establishment (Boston: Beacon Press, 1964).

Religion, The State and the Schools (New York: Pegasus, 1967).

American Empire: The Political Ethics of Twentieth Century Conquest (New York: Macmillan, 1970).

Libertation Ethics (New York: Macmillan, 1972).

The Politics of Liberation (Elgin, IL.: The Brethren Press, 1984).

El Poder Militar in Los Estados Unidos (a translation of *The Military Establishment* (S.A./Mexico, Ediciones ERA, 1964).

PUBLICATIONS – CHAPTERS

Chapter, "Government Chaplaincies," James E. Wood, Editor, *Religion and the State: Essays in Honor of Leo Pfeffer* (Waco, Texas: Baylor University Press, 1985).

Chapter 4, "Myths of Soviet Intentions," Editor, Dale W. Brown, *What About the Russians* (Elgin, Illinois: The Brethren Press, 1984).

Chapter 8, "A Human Life Amendment Violates Constitutional Rights," Editors, Bruno Leone, Teresa O'Neill, Claudia Debner, Connie Szumski, *Death/Dying – Opposing Viewpoints: Sources* (St. Paul, Minnesota: Greenhaven Press, 1984)

Chapter 11, "Amnesty: The Record and Need," Editors, Paul T. Jersild, Dale A. Johnson, *Moral Issues and Christian Response* (New York: Holt, Rinehart and Winston, 1976).

"Our Only Security," Sermon on Armed Forces Day, Editor, Alton M. Motter, *Preaching on National Holidays* (Philadelphia: Fortress Press, 1976).

Introduction to Kirby Page, *Now Is the Time to Prevent A Third World War*, in Garland Library of War and Peace Edition (1972).

Introduction to Cecil John Cadoux, *Christian Pacifism Re-examined*, in Garland Library of War and Peace Edition (1972).

Chapter 2, "Abortion and Civil Liberty," *Abortion: A Human Choice* (Washington, D.C., Board of Christian Social Concerns, The United Methodist Church, 1971).

Chapter, "The Military Industrial Alliance," Editor, Neal D. Houghton, *Struggle Against History: U.S. Foreign Policy in an Age of Revolution* (New York, Washington Square Press, 1968).

Chapter, *The Situation Ethics Debate*, Editor, Harvey Cox, (Philadelphia, Westminster Press, 1968).

Chapter, "The Dangers of the Draft," Editors, Robert P. Friedman and Charley Leistner, *The Forensic Quarterly: Compulsory Service Systems* (Columbia, Missouri National University Extension Association, 1968).

Chapter 5, "The Growth of Military Influence," Editor, Daniel E. Taylor, *Peace and Power* (Nashville, Parthenon Press, 1960).

Chapter 2, "Christian Dynamic for Social Change," *The Word of God in the Nuclear Age* (New York, Church Peace Mission, 1959).

Chapter 1, "The Problem of Security," Editor, Paul Poling, *Let Us Live for God and the Nations: A Study and Action Guide For Christians in World Affairs* (Philadelphia, Country Life Press for Board of Christian Education, Presbyterian Church in the U.S.A., 1951).

Chapter, "Civil Defense and Conscription," Chapter, "An Army Mistake," Editor, Bower Aly, *The NUEA Debate Handbook*, Volume 1, *War Service* (Columbia, Mo. National University Extension Association, 1951-52).

PUBLICATIONS – REPORTS

Co-Author, *The Draft*, A report prepared for the Peace Education Division of the American Friends Service Committee (New York, Hill and Wang, 1968)

Co-Author, *In Place of War: An Inquiry Into Non Violent National Defense* (New York, Grossman Publishers, 1967)

PUBLICATIONS – MONOGRAPHS

The Militarization of America, A report prepared for the National Council Against Conscription and release by Albert Einstein, Ray Lyman Wilbur, Dorothy Canfield Fisher and 18 others (Washington, NCAC, 1948) 32 pages.

New Evidence of the Militarization of America, A report prepared for the National Council Against Conscription and released by Pearl Buck, Albert Einstein, Victor Reuther, W. J. Miller S.J. and others (Washington, NCAC, 1949) 64 pages.

Militarism in Education, A report prepared for the National Council Against Conscription and released by Albert Einstein, Pitirim Sorokin, Alonzo F. Myers and 23 other educators and authors. (Washington, NCAC, 1950) 80 pages.

America, Russia and the Bomb, A report prepared for the National Council Against Conscription and released by Albert Einstein, Louis Bromfield, Benjamin E. Mays and 13 others. (Washington, NCAC, 1950) 72 pages.

Press Agents of the Pentagon, A study of the publicity methods of Department of Defense, (Washington, National Council Against Conscription, 1953) 60 pages.

The Peace Offensive and the Cold War, A study of Communist political theory and strategy related to the cold war. (Washington, National Council Against Conscription, 1954) 38 pages.

Church, State and Education, (New York, National Council of Churches, 1964).

MAJOR POLITICAL ACTIVITY

Lobbied for Methodist World Peace Commission against World War II draft, 1940.

Meeting with three others with Eleanor Roosevelt in Hyde Park, N.Y. to discuss rights for conscientious objectors in draft legislation, September 1940.

171

Organized Committee Against Jim Crow in Military Training and Service, November 1947, which was influential in securing desegration of the armed forces.

Organized campaign which resulted in Congressional investigation, 1947, of War Department public relations and propaganda.

Debate with Major General Lewis B. Hershey, Director of Selective Service, on the American Forum of the Air, on subject "Do We Need U.M.T. Now." The debate was televised nationally but originated in Wardman Park Hotel ballroom with a number of members of Congress present, February 1952.

As Executive Secretary of the Fellowship of Reconciliation provided and financed a staff member, Glenn Smiley, to assist Martin Luther King during the Montgomery Bus Boycott, 1956.

Participated with Glenn Smiley in Atlanta in strategy meeting with Martin Luther King, Ralph Abernathy and two black leaders from each deep Southern state regarding south-wide action, 1956.

Participated with A. J. Muste and three others from Fellowship of Reconciliation in series of dialogue meetings with five top Communists, 1956.

Meeting in Prague with National Liberation Front representative from Vietnam on behalf of F.O.R. and anti-war movement to discuss sending U.S. delegations to Vietnam, 1966.

Meeting with East German Minister of Church-State Affairs in Berlin, 1966 and with Dr. Heinz Kloppenberg who had asked me to convince the Minister that the German churches were not tools of the American churches and the U.S. churches were not tools of the U.S. Government. This resulted in permission to send certain West German church books and periodicals into East Germany.

Addressed the Foreign Affairs Committee, British House of Commons, 1966 on invitation of its Chair, Philip Noel-Baker on topic, "Can Britain Help Get the U.S. out of the War in Vietnam?"

Prepared "Amnesty: The Record and Need" as a study guide and organized an effort for amnesty among peace groups and churches, 1969.

Negotiated on behalf of the American Indian Movement with Department of Justice personnel at Wounded Knee for non-violent ending of confrontation, 1973. The attempt was unsuccessful.

Joined with Senator Jovito Salonga to organize ecumenically a church-state confrontation using non-violent resistance to the Marcos dictatorship, 1973.

Secured official permission as first foreigner to visit and investigate conditions in Philippine concentration camps and submit report to Commander of the Philippine Constabulary, 1973.

Visited Nicaragua and Honduras, April 1983. Returned to U.S. to persuade F.O.R. and other groups to make opposition to U.S. intervention in Central America a major program.

Testified before U.S. Senate and House Military Affairs Committees, beginning in 1940, and also House and Senate Armed Services Committees, the House Ways and Means Committee, the Senate Foreign Relations Committee and others through 1984.

SPECIAL LECTURES

Conception Theological Seminary, Benedictine Abbey, Conception, Mo., October 1962. Topic: Pacifism.

Conference of Scholars on Cold War and Communism, Estes Park, March 1967, Topic: The Military Industrial Alliance.

Conference of Army and Reserve Chaplains, 3rd Army, Ft. McPherson, Georgia, October 1967. Topic: Moral Issues in Conscription.

University of Mississippi Law School, Jackson, Mississippi, March 1968. Topic: Dissent and Civil Disobedience.

Roman Catholic Theological Seminary, Cordoba, Argentina, 1969. Topic: Liberation by Violence or Non-Violence.

Gandhi Peace Foundation, New Delhi, India, 1973. Four lectures: Justice, Revolution, and Violence; the U.S. Civil Rights Movement; Non-violence and Education; The Military Industrial Complex.

Silliman University, Dumagete, Philippines, September, 1973. Topics: Liberation and Violence; the Civil Rights Movement in the U.S.; A Critical Appraisal of U.S Foreign Policy.

Union Theological Seminary and Philippine Christian College, October 1973, Series of four lectures on Liberation.

Putnam Lecture, Hamline University, St. Paul, Minnesota, March 1974. Topic: Violence and Social Change.

Willamette University School of Law, Salem, Oregon, April 1974. Topic: Amnesty.

Huston Memorial Peace Lecture, Bethany Theological Seminary, Oak Brook, Illinois, May 1977. Topic: War and Revolution in Christian Perspective.

Chautauqua Institution, New York, Summer, 1980. Five lectures: Religion and the Politics of Peace.

Paine lectures, University of Missouri, Columbia, Missouri, 1980. Topic: Latin American Theologies of Liberation.

Vanderbilt University, Nashville, Tennessee, March 1981. Topic: National Security in the Nuclear Age.

University of Southern California, Annenberg School, May 1981. Topic: Conscience in U.S. History.

Chautauqua Institution, New York, Summer 1981. Five Lectures: Theology of Liberation: the Politics of Freedom.

Baptist Joint Committee on Public Affairs, Annual Assembly, Washington, D.C., Topic: Creationism and Evolution.

COLLEGE AND SEMINARY SPEAKING

Lectured or addressed faculty or students at many colleges and universities throughout the United States including the following: Dartmouth, Colby, Bowdoin, Harvard, Wellesley, Amherst, Holy Cross, Brown, University of New Hampshire, Hobart, Oberlin, Swarthmore, Lafayette, Pennsylvania State, Ohio State, Ohio Wesleyan, Fisk, Lewis and Clark, Reed, University of Hawaii, University of California at Riverside, Sacramento State University, Washington State, University of Washington, Montana State, Iowa State, Iowa Wesleyan, Nebraska Wesleyan, University of Kansas, Gonzaga, Duke, University of North Carolina.

Among the theological schools are the following: Boston University, Yale Divinity School, Union (New York), General, Colgate-Rochester, McCormick, Garrett, Crozier, Vanderbilt, Bethany, Associated Mennonite Seminaries, Duke, Perkins, Iliff, Bonebrake, United Methodist, Wesley, Christian (Indianapolis), Phillips, United (Minnesota), St. Johns, Conception, Dubuque, Wartburg, Concordia, Seminex, Southern Baptist (Louisville), Eden, Gammon, Louisville Presbyterian, Claremont, Pacific School of Religion, Andover Newton, Earlham.

SUMMAR SCHOOL TEACHING

University of Kansas Medical Center, Kansas City, Kansas, June 1975, "Ethical Issues in BioMedicine."

University of the Pacific, Stockton, California, 1975, "Alternatives for Social Change in the U.S. and the Third World."

University of Kansas Medical Center, Kansas City, Kansas, June 1976, "Ethical Issues in BioMedicine."

Iliff School of Theology, Denver, Colorado, 1979, "The Process of Peace in World Affairs."

Wisconsin State University System: College Faculty Seminar, June 1981, "Educating for Freedom."

TRAVEL

Lecturer daily on International Relations and Travel Tips for European Countries on Greek Luxury Liner Olympia, New York to Athens, Summer 1955.

Resource leader of Latin American Seminar on Revolution, Executive Tour sponsored by the Christian Church (Disciples of Christ) Summer 1970.

Resource leader and lecturer on Soviet-American Relations, and Armaments Issues, Peace Cruise on the Volga, July 24-August 16, 1984, sponsored by four U.S. peace organizations.

Travel in the following countries:

China, Pakistan, Nepal, Ceylon, Burma, Malayasia, Singapore, Philippines.

Japan, Hong Kong. Three visits.

Mexico. Five visits.

Guatemala. Three visits.

Honduras, Costa Rica, Panama, Columbia, Venezuela. Two visits.

Nicaragua, Ecuador, Peru, Bolivia, Brazil, Chile, Uruguay, Argentina, Cuba, Jamaica, Tobago, Puerto Rico.

Republic of South Africa, Botswana, Rhodesia, Zambia, Tanzania, Kenya, Ethiopia, Nigeria, Gabon, Cameroons, Liberia, Algeria, Tangiers, Egypt.

Israel. Two visits.

Syria, Cyprus, Jordan, Lebanon, Iraq, Turkey.

Greece. Three visits.

Soviet Union, Yugoslavia, Czechoslovakia, Austria, Sweden, Poland.

Finland, East Germany. Two visits.

Spain-4, Portugal-2, Italy-3, France-8, Germany-8, Netherlands-10, Switzerland-3, Luxembourg-3, United Kingdom-12, Denmark-4, Belgium-4.

Canada-5, fifty U.S. states.

ARTICLES IN PERIODICALS

"Action Program for Campus Pacifists," *Fellowship*, September 1, 1940.

"Pacifist Youth News and Plans," *Fellowship*, November, 1940.

"Christian View of Compulsory Military Training," *The Debate Hand-book*, 1941.

"Training for Compulsory Patriotism," *Motive*, March, 1945.

"Should Patriotism Be Compulsory?" *Zion's Herald*, March 7, 1945.

"The Future Belongs to Peace," *Motive*, April, 1945.

"International Abolition of Peacetime Conscription," *Motive*, October, 1945.

"The Root of Militarism," *Gospel Messenger*, October 27, 1945.

"Pearl Harbor and Preparedness," *Fellowship*, November, 1945.

"The Aim of Conscription is Indoctrination," *Friends Intelligencer*, Twelfth Month, One, 1945.

"The Cost of Peacetime Military Training," *The American Friend*, January 10, 1946.

"Consider Conscription Carefully," *Zion's Herald*, January 30, 1946.

"Conscription in the Atomic Age," *Motive*, February, 1946.

"The Legion's 'Painless' Peacetime Draft," *Fellowship*, March, 1946.

"Does Preparedness Really Prepare?" *Gospel Messenger*, January 11, 1947.

Guest editorial on conscription in *Denver Post*, December 30, 1947.

"Disarmament, the Road to Peace"—Booklet, British Fellowship of Reconciliation, 1947.

"President's Commission on Universal Military Training," *The American Friend*, January 22, 1948.

"Shall We Construct or Conscript?" *Montana Education*, January, 1948.

"Heads for Brass Hats," *Intercollegian*, March, 1949.

"Deathblows from a Mirage," *Motive*, March, 1949.

"Alliance of Insecurity," *Fellowship*, June, 1949.

"Israel's Future," *Fellowship*, March, 1950.

"Total Disarmament or Total War," *Fellowship*, May, 1950.

"Shall They Learn War?" *Social Progress*, December, 1950.

"The Whole Truth," *Discovery*, July-September, 1950.

"We Can Still Defeat U.M.T.," *Fellowship*, January, 1951.

"Asia in the World," *Fellowship*, March, 1951.

"Why I Oppose Universal Military Service," *Christian Advocate*, September 20, 1951.

"War's Tinderbox—The Middle East," *Fellowship*, October, 1951.

"Is It Police Action?" *Zion's Herald*, December 26, 1951.

"U.M.T., Denial of Democracy," *Social Progress*, January, 1952.

"On the Rim of Russia," *Fellowship*, January, 1952.

"The Eisenhower Portent," *Christian Century*, January 30, 1952.

"The New Meaning of 'Universal'," *Zion's Herald*, February 27, 1952.

"What About Iran?" *Zion's Herald*, March 26, 1952.

"Visit to Berlin," *Reconciliation*, magazine of British Fellowship of Reconciliation, April, 1952.

"U.M.T.," *International Fellowship of Reconciliation Newsletter*, June, 1952.

"An American View of Britain," *Reconciliation*, August, 1952.

"Surface Tension," *Fellowship*, December, 1952.

"The Pacifist and the Legion," *Fellowship*, January, 1953.

"The Pacifist and the American Legion," *Peace News*, May 22, 1953, London, England.

"The Struggle for Power," *Fellowship*, December, 1953.

"A Post-Liberal Pacifism," *Fellowship*, February, 1954.

"A Leaven Within the Church," *Fellowship*, April, 1954.

"The Threat of Militarism," *Motive*, April, 1954.

"Can't We Sit Down and Discuss It?" *Fellowship*, July, 1954.

"Letters from the U.S.A.," *Peace News*, London, July 9 and July 16, 1954.

"Conscription in the U.S.," *Conscientious Objection to Conscription*, International Fellowship of Reconciliation, London, 1955.

"Universal—Compulsory—Permanent," *Fellowship*, March, 1955.

"Facts About Universal Training-Compulsory Reserve Proposal," *Commercial and Financial Chronicle*, March 17, 1955.

"The Risks in Disarmament," *Christian Advocate*, July 8, 1955.

"Note from Pakistan," *Fellowship*, February, 1956.

"Palliatives Will Not Do," *Fellowship*, March 1, 1958.

"The End of Conscription Is Overdue," *Friends Committee on National Legislation Newsletter*, November, 1958.

"End Conscription in 1959!" *Christian Century*, January 7, 1959.

"The Growing Power of the Military," *Progressive*, January, 1959.

"The Army Gets Its Way," *Progressive*, April, 1959.

"The Army Gets Its Way," *Motive*, October, 1959.

"America Needs a Revolutionary Strategy," *Progressive*, January, 1960.

"The Case for Disarmament," *Progressive*, April, 1960.

"Myths About Communist China," *Motive*, May, 1960.

"Total Versus Partial Disarmament," *Arunodayan* (India), July, 1960.

"Our Commissioned Clergymen," *Fellowship*, September 1, 1960.

"The Right Wing Extremists," *Fellowship*, June 15, 1961.

"Communism and Coexistence," *Fellowship*, July, 1961.

"Berlin: Background of a Crisis," *Minority of One*, September, 1961.

"Berlin Crisis," *Tabloid American*, November, 1961.

"Civil Defense: Is It Defense or Preparation for War?" *Christian Advocate*, February 1, 1962.

"Military Influence in U.S.A.: How Much?" *Christian Action*, July, 1962.

"Communists at Odds," *Concern*, August 15, 1962.

"The Chinese-Indian Border War," *Concern*, May 1, 1963.

"The Missouri School-Bus Debate," *Christian Advocate*, August 15, 1963.

"Situation du Mouvement Pacifiste parmi Les Protestants," *Christianisme Social* (Paris), Septembre-Decembre, 1963.

"Civil Rights and the Extreme Left and Right," address presented at Missouri Association for Social Welfare, Annual Conference 1964 abstracted in SCAN (Short Conference Abstract Notes).

Response to "Let's Talk About Berlin," *Fellowship*, March, 1964.

"Goldwater: Yes or No?" Response from seven Protestant clergymen, *Christian Century*, July, 1964.

"Service as a Conscientious Objector," *Classmate*, September, 1964.

"Military und Politik in U.S.A.," *Zurcher Woche* (Zurich), October 30, 1964.

"The War in Vietnam," *Concern*, December 1, 1964.

"The Limited Objectors," *Christian Century*, December 15, 1965.

"The Right to Dissent," *Christian Advocate*, January 28, 1966.

"The Military's Growing Powers Since Vietnam," *Fellowship*, March, 1966.

"What Chance for Religious Freedom in Spain?" *Christian Century*, May 18, 1966.

"Revolution und Gewaltlosigkeit," *Junge Kirche* (Dortmund) July 10, 1966.

"An Interview with the NLF," *War/Peace Report*, August-September, 1966.

"A Christian-Marxist Conversation," *Christian Century*, September 21, 1966.

"World Opinion and Vietnam: The Fear of United States Policy," *The Churchman*, October, 1966.

"Differing Christian Approaches in East Germany," *Christian Advocate*, October 6, 1966.

"Situation Ethics," *Fellowship*, November, 1966.

"Justice, Revolution, and Violence," *Reconciliation Quarterly*, International Fellowship of Reconciliation, third quarter, 1966.

"The National Service Proposal," *Christian Century*, January 11, 1967.

"If the Vietnam War Escalates Into China: Consequences Inside the U.S.," *Minority of One*, January, 1967.

"Twenty-five Years of Conscription," *Chrisitian Century*, April 12, 1967.

"Danger of Global War Grows with Escalation," *The Mennonite*, June 6, 1967.

"Conscience and the Draft," *Christian Century*, June 28, 1967.

"Peacetime Military Conscription," *Journal of Gandhi Peace Foundation*, July, 1967.

"The Administration's Hopes: Surrender Abroad, Capitulation at Home," *Fellowship*, July, 1967.

"The Kansas City Riot Could Have Been Averted," *Focus/Midwest*, Vol. 6, No. 42, 1968.

"1967 Viet Elections Analyzed," *U.S. Farm News*, January, 1968.

"The Vietnam War Tax," *Christian Century*, February 7, 1968.

"Who Speaks for the Church?" *Christian Century*, March 6, 1968.

"Extremism and Christianity," *Christian Advocate*, April 18, 1968.

"Economic Bases of the Cold War," *Christian Century*, May 1, 1968.

"Conscience and the Draft," *Christian Century*, June 28, 1968.

"What LBJ Seeks in Paris," *National Catholic Reporter*, August 14, 1968.

"Peace Negotiations of President Johnson," *Minority of One*, September, 1968.

"Draft Exiles in Canada," *Christian Century*, October 30, 1968.

"Memo to Nixon: Why Not an Amnesty?" *National Catholic Reporter*, January 1, 1969.

"China's Cultural Revolution," *New World Outlook*, January, 1969.

"Escalatie in oorlogen economie gaan hand in hand," *Militia Christi* (Netherlands), January 25, 1969.

"Pax Americana," *Christian Advocate*, March 6, 1969.

"America as a Militaristic Society," *The Catholic World*, August, 1969.

"Ecumenism and the School Aid Issue," *Christian Century*, August 11, 1969.

"How Popular Is Uncle Sam Around the World?" *Face to Face*, October, 1969.

"Argentina Methodists Became Autonomous," *Christian Century*, November 12, 1969.

"Labor Repression in Argentina," *Christian Century*, December 3, 1969.

"Civil Liberties in Agentina," *Fellowship*, January, 1970.

"Little West Points," *Engage*, August 1 & 15, 1970.

"Parochial Schools Need More Than Money," *Christian Herald*, September, 1970.

"Latin America," *World Call*, October, 1970.

"Who Wants Catholic Schools?" *Nation*, December 14, 1970.

"Pacifism in Church History," Survey for Westminster Dictionary of Church History, 1971.

"Are Parochial Schools Imperiled?" *Christian Century*, January 13, 1971.

"The Draft: What Is Its Future?" *Face to Face*, February, 1971.

"Victory for Church-State Separation," *The Churchman*, March, 1971.

"The Time Has Come to End the Draft," *Face to Face*, April, 1971.

"What Is the Real Issue?" *Christian Advocate*, April 15, 1971.

"Aid to Parochial Schools," *Christian Advocate*, April 17, 1971.

"Taproot of Militarism," *Engage*, May 15, 1971.

"The Draft and Its Mythology," *Courage*, June, 1971.

"Parochiaid and Texas," *Christian Century*, September 1, 1971.

"False Parochial School Argument," *The Churchman*, September, 1971.

"That Calley Case," *Fellowship*, September, 1971.

"Vouchers Pose a Threat to Public Schools," *Christian Advocate*, September 16, 1971.

"Are Parochial Schools Imperiled?," *Liberty*, September-October, 1971.

"Outler's Position on Abortion," *Christian Advocate*, November, 1971.

"Mr. Nixon, China and Japan," *Fellowship*, December, 1971.

"The Illusion of Nixonomics," *Fellowship*, February, 1972.

"America's Private Empire," *Fellowship*, February, 1972.

"400% of U.S. Profits Angering Latin Americans," *Fellowship*, March, 1972.

"Jesus a Resister?" *Fellowship*, April, 1972.

"Friends Are Free People," *Sign, National Catholic Magazine*, May, 1972.

"Church, State and Mr. Nixon," *Nation*, September 11, 1972.

"Human Sexuality and Public Policy," *Engage*, December, 1972.

"Amnesty and Reconciliation," *Christian Century*, December 27, 1972.

"Surrounded by Heavy Weapons, Indians Appealed to the F.O.R." report of reconciliation trip to Wounded Knee, *Fellowship*, Spring, 1973.

"Should Tax Credits Support Parochial Schools?" *Christian Advocate*, May 24, 1973.

"Anti-Abortion Amendment Threatens Religious Freedom," *Christian Advocate*, September 27, 1973.

"Polarization in the Philippines," *Nation*, January 26, 1974.

"Militarism Returns to Japan," *Christian Century*, February 13, 1974.

"Richard Gregg," *Fellowship*, April, 1974.

"Overpopulation and the Hunger Crisis," *Christian Century*, May 22, 1974.

"Japan's Policy, the New Militarism," *Intellectual Digest*, June, 1974.

"The Political Power of Multi-National Corporations," *Christian Century*, September 25, 1974.

"Inside Marcos's Concentration Camps," *Christian Century*, November 13, 1974.

"Accused, the Oil Companies," *Focus/Midwest*, Vol. 9, No. 61, 1974.

"Cardinal Krol, Parochiad and the Jews," *Christian Century*, December 17, 1975.

"Detente and Disarmament," *Christian Century*, March 17, 1976.

"The U.S. Role in Asia's Future," *Christian Century*, September 29, 1976.

"Abortion and the Law," *Church and State*, November, 1976.

"The Case Against the C.I.A.," *Fellowship*, December, 1976.

"Exploding the Deterrence Theory," *Sojourners*, February, 1977.

"Disarmament Begins at Home," *National Catholic Reporter*, April 8, 1977.

"Black Rule in Rhodesia Won't Exclude Churches," *National Catholic Reporter*, July 15, 1977.

"The War System Is the Enemy," *Fellowship*, October, 1977.

"Ambassador: Here's a Vibrant Church," *National Catholic Reporter*, October 21, 1977.

"John Nevin Sayre: Peacemaker," *Fellowship*, November, 1977.

"South African Crackdown May Herald Tighter Controls," *National Catholic Reporter*, November 11, 1977.

"Archbishop: Mixed Race Schools in South Africa Face Obstacles," *National Catholic Reporter*, November 18, 1977.

"Capetown Housing Bad for Blacks," *National Catholic Reporter*, December 16, 1977.

"Christianity in Africa: Churches Fight Racism Differently," *National Catholic Reporter*, December 16, 1977.

"What It's Like in Rhodesia Today," *Nation*, January 7-14, 1978.

"Survey: Africa Grants Wide Religious Freedom," *National Catholic Reporter*, January 13, 1978.

"Marxist Moves Parallel Missioners," *National Catholic Reporter*, February 3, 1978.

"Christian Effect on Racism Limited," *National Catholic Reporter*, February 17, 1978.

"Refugees Trade Security for Freedom," *National Catholic Reporter*, February 24, 1978.

"Money Won't Sway South Africa," *National Catholic Reporter*, March 3, 1978.

"Peace Conversion," *Fellowship*, April/May, 1978.

"John Nevin Sayre: A Ministry of Reconciliation," *Fellowship*, June, 1978.

"F.O.R.: Looking Back on 63 Years," *Fellowship*, November, 1978.

"John Nevin Sayre: The War Years," *Fellowship*, January/February, 1979.

"John Nevin Sayre: Binding Up the Wounds," *Fellowship*, November, 1979.

"Punish in Corrective or Rehabilitative Way," *Engage/Social Action*, January, 1980.

"C.O.'s and Draft Registration," *Christian Century*, July 16-23, 1980.

"The Lack of Concern About Smoking Ethics," *Engage/Social Action*, September, 1980.

"Christian Worship of Violence," Address to Sewanee Disarmament Conference, in *Saint Luke's Journal of Theology*, September, 1980.

"The Catholic League: Civil Rights or Sectarian Pressure?" *Church and State*, October, 1980.

"Too Many Blacks? The All-Volunteer Force," *Christian Century*, October 1, 1980.

"The Decade Ahead in Church-State Issues," *Christian Century*, Febru-ary 25, 1981.

"The Holy War Mentality," *Fellowship*, April-May, 1981.

"Politican Realism and National Security," *National Institute for Campus Ministries Journal*, Spring, 1981.

"No Angels, No Devils," Essay in *Confrontation*, a literary journal of Long Island University, Winter, 1981.

"Conscience Versus the Draft," *Christianity and Crisis*, November 15, 1982.

"Setting the Record Straight," *Fellowship*, December, 1982.

"U.S. Double Standard Nicaragua's Chief Foe," *National Catholic Reporter*, June 3, 1983.

"Public Schools Embattled over Prayer," *Christian Century*, July 20-27, 1983.

"Secular Humanism — Neutral Ground for Teaching Values," *Report from the Capitol*, July-August, 1983.

"The American Education Debate," *Christian Century*, August-September 7, 1983.

"The Undeclared War Against Nicaragua," *Fellowship*, July-August, 1983.

"Fact-Finding in Nicaragua," *The Churchman*, August-September, 1983.

"A Toe Hold for Religion in Public Education," *Christian Century*, February 15, 1984.

"Required Recitation Can't Be Voluntary," *Kansas City Star*, Star Forum section, March 11, 1984.

"Holy See Diplomacy," *The Churchman*, April-May, 1984.

"Statement on Behalf of the American Civil Liberties Union," *U.S. Farm News*, May, 1984.

"Roman Bishops Overlook Vital Points," *The Churchman*, March, 1985.

Politics Centered Upon Abortion," *The Churchman*, April, 1985.

"Consent of the Governed — Silence," *The Churchman*, June-July, 1985.

"Church and State in Poland," *Christian Century*, July 31-August 7, 1985.

"The Lessons of Solidarity," *Fellowship* July-August, 1985.